T0373028

BELIEFISM

Also by Paul Dolan:

Happiness by Design
Happy Ever After

BELIEFISM

How to stop hating the people we disagree with

Paul Dolan

The
Bridge
Street
Press

THE BRIDGE STREET PRESS

First published in Great Britain in 2025 by The Bridge Street Press

1 3 5 7 9 10 8 6 4 2

A CIP catalogue record for this book
is available from the British Library.

ISBN 978-0-349-12869-6

Typeset in Bembo by M Rules
Printed and bound in Great Britain by
Clays Ltd, Elcograf S.p.A.

Papers used by The Bridge Street Press are from well-managed forests
and other responsible sources.

MIX
Paper | Supporting
responsible forestry
FSC® C104740

The Bridge Street Press
An imprint of
Little, Brown Book Group
Carmelite House
50 Victoria Embankment
London EC4Y 0DZ

The authorised representative
in the EEA is
Hachette Ireland
8 Castlecourt Centre
Dublin 15, D15 XTP3, Ireland
(email: info@hbgi.ie)

An Hachette UK Company
www.hachette.co.uk

www.littlebrown.co.uk

Contents

Part 1: Taking Sides

Part 2: Breaking Sides

Part 3: Picking Sides

Part 1

Taking Sides

1

The road to beliefism

The company we keep

'Some of my best friends are black.' This was a phrase used by white people until a decade or so ago to suggest they were not racist. It is largely an empty claim. Having black friends does not in itself mean that someone is not racist. Having a girl-friend does not make a man any less sexist. More than that, the phrase was often used to justify having said something or having acted in a way that *was* racist. It was intended as a 'get out of jail free' card against accusations of being racist when, in fact, it had the opposite effect. As a result, it quite quickly became seen as a sign of being racist. There are data from the US showing that this is how black Americans interpreted the term,[1] and I can certainly recall plenty of people of all races in the UK mocking it as a phrase only used by apologists for racism.

But perhaps we shouldn't be so quick to mock. I think it's fair to say, all else equal, that a white person with black friends would be less racist than a white person with no black friends at all. Similarly, all else equal – and that is the important term here – a man with female friends is likely to be less sexist than a man with no female friends at all. It is true that signalling you have black friends if you are white can be used to license racist comments and behaviours but very few white people will have black friends only to provide 'cover' for speaking or acting in racist ways. Having black friends that are 'genuine' is a behaviour that signals relatively more tolerance than having no black friends at all. As the Japanese proverb says: 'When the character of a person is not clear, look at their friends.'

Consider social class, which has always fascinated me given that I grew up in social housing and now work in academia. Leaving to one side the challenges of defining social class, I know plenty of academics who no longer have any friends from the 'working-class world' they grew up around. In contrast, most of my best friends would be defined as working class by standard markers of occupation and income (and some are middle class). I think that this matters, for at least two reasons. First, I have direct access to what it means to be working class in the modern world in a way that those who have only middle-class friends do not. Second, I have chosen to remain deeply connected to one 'world' while joining the ranks of another. Most people from working-class backgrounds who gain social status become disconnected from the groups they were once part of. All else equal, this must mean that I am more tolerant of class differences than they are. I am less classist, right?

If you're not convinced by this somewhat simplistic exposition, consider the beliefs of someone's friends. Would you conclude that someone who only had friends with the same set of beliefs was less tolerant than someone who had friends with different beliefs? What if they believed in the sanctity of marriage, say, and refused to be friends with someone who believed in polyamory? If you surround yourself only with people who share similar views to you, then you are, by definition, discriminating against those who disagree – this is *beliefism*. The more you discriminate, the more beliefist you are. Beliefism can be seen as a strong form of intolerance. Someone who is beliefist is not only intolerant of people and perspectives that are different to theirs, but this spills over into them actively avoiding people who disagree. A beliefist may pass someone over for a job, say, because they only want to hire people who share similar beliefs on issues that matter to them.

Logically, there is no difference between racism, sexism, classism, beliefism or any other 'ism' in this regard. Clearly, we can quite legitimately choose to be intolerant of people who are themselves intolerant. We care about integrity as well as tolerance, and we are certainly under no obligation to be friends with someone who is racist, sexist, classist – or beliefist. There is no moral value to the claim that some of my best friends are racist. But when we use someone's (different but not abhorrent) beliefs on one issue to completely dismiss them, and all their other beliefs, we are guilty of using a tiny fraction of information about that person to judge their whole character. An 'ism' in the sense it is used here is a discrim-inatory belief, and so beliefism can sit alongside any of the other isms that are used quickly to categorise people in ways that are unjust.

This is a book about beliefism. And how to reduce it. I am strongly of the view that the world would be a better place if there was less beliefism and more tolerance of different perspectives and the people that hold them. There would be less conflict and more economic and social progress. Unlike a lot of what has been written about political polarisation, it is not my ambition to reduce extreme views.[2] Indeed, I have no intention of changing your mind about anything except how you interact with those who have different beliefs. I'm going to put forward my own beliefs in this book and I would obviously like it if you agreed with me. But much more than that, I hope that you will still want to engage with me if you disagree.

Well-functioning societies embrace a wide range of perspectives.[3] Some of the most profound advances in knowledge have come from those who were thought to have extreme, even crazy, views at the time. Consider the monumental shifts brought about by Galileo Galilei's heliocentric view of our universe and Albert Einstein's theory of relativity. These and other figures underline the importance of outlier perspectives in enhancing our collective wisdom. Moreover, there is also some evidence to suggest that economic and social progress requires that the consensus gets challenged from time to time in stable democracies which would otherwise face the risk of capture from special interest groups.[4] This view has not gone uncontested, but it does alert us to the potential need for shocks to the system to loosen the grip of vested interests.

We currently face radical uncertainty, e.g., around artificial intelligence (AI), and this makes it even more important that we reduce beliefism and listen to the outliers. Can anyone confidently claim to know what's going to happen next with generative AI? It makes no sense to ignore anyone's views about it. Decision making in households, corporations and institutions could all be enhanced by a greater willingness to listen to different perspectives and people. A reduction in beliefism will also serve to take the heat out of interactions with those who disagree with us. I'm editing this paragraph the day after the attempted assassination of Donald Trump in July 2024. While assassinations and attempted assassinations of US presidents are not without precedent, in many ways, yesterday's event and all the context and circumstances surrounding it can be seen as the perfect illustration of contemporary beliefism. It certainly provides considerable motivation to reduce it, and not just in the US.

By being less beliefist at a personal level and on a day-to-day basis, you might be a better partner or parent, or a more effective buddy or boss. Well-rounded individuals accept and respect different perspectives and people. Being less beliefist will broaden your horizons, so that you are smarter, and have stronger and more fulfilling relationships. Overall, you'll be happier. But perhaps not immediately so, as you adjust to listening to different perspectives outside your comfort zone. Being less beliefist can be quite a challenge and disagreement is hard to deal with. There will be provocations in this book that you can use to think and act differently irrespective of your baseline degree of beliefism.

If you tolerate this ...

This is a book about beliefism in general, and not only in politics. Some meat eaters dislike and seek to avoid vegans, and vice versa. Some very healthy people distance themselves from sedentary people, and vice versa. The list goes on. People segregate themselves from, and have a considerable degree of hostility towards, others who think and act differently. How many of these things really matter to you? And if they do, does it result in you avoiding and/or showing hostility towards the 'other side'? To consider this further, please look at the list of issues overleaf and rate how much you would want to avoid someone based on them having polar opposite views to you. Come on, be honest ...

	Not avoid at all						Completely avoid			
Music taste	0	1	2	3	4	5	6	7	8	9	10
Alcohol consumption	0	1	2	3	4	5	6	7	8	9	10
Illicit drug use	0	1	2	3	4	5	6	7	8	9	10
Tattoos	0	1	2	3	4	5	6	7	8	9	10
Abortion	0	1	2	3	4	5	6	7	8	9	10
Religion	0	1	2	3	4	5	6	7	8	9	10
Veganism	0	1	2	3	4	5	6	7	8	9	10
Swearing	0	1	2	3	4	5	6	7	8	9	10
Environmental issues	0	1	2	3	4	5	6	7	8	9	10
Sportiness	0	1	2	3	4	5	6	7	8	9	10
Humour	0	1	2	3	4	5	6	7	8	9	10
Immigration	0	1	2	3	4	5	6	7	8	9	10
Football team	0	1	2	3	4	5	6	7	8	9	10
Trans rights	0	1	2	3	4	5	6	7	8	9	10
Political affiliation	0	1	2	3	4	5	6	7	8	9	10
Emotional expressiveness	0	1	2	3	4	5	6	7	8	9	10
Economic equality	0	1	2	3	4	5	6	7	8	9	10
Freedom of speech	0	1	2	3	4	5	6	7	8	9	10
Marriage	0	1	2	3	4	5	6	7	8	9	10
Monogamy	0	1	2	3	4	5	6	7	8	9	10
How to bring up kids	0	1	2	3	4	5	6	7	8	9	10

Would you like to know how you compare to the general population? Well, in April 2024 we ran a survey with 500 adults in the UK. The average level of 'avoidance' across all questions was 3.3, with a quarter of responses below 2.0 and a quarter above 4.8. There are also some big differences across questions, of course – see the figure opposite. Our sample is pretty tolerant of people who support a different football team, have different taste in music and different views about tattoos, sportiness and marriage. The sample really wants to avoid those with different views on drugs. With a mean 'avoid score' of 7 out of 10, it's over two points higher than trans rights in second place. How do you compare with the UK average? Are you generally more or less beliefist than the average Brit?

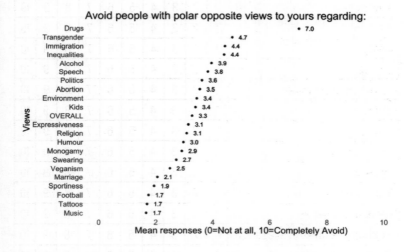

Avoid people with polar opposite views to yours regarding:

Views	Mean responses (0=Not at all, 10=Completely Avoid)
Drugs	7.0
Transgender	4.7
Immigration	4.4
Inequalities	4.4
Alcohol	3.9
Speech	3.8
Politics	3.6
Abortion	3.5
Environment	3.4
Kids	3.4
OVERALL	3.3
Expressiveness	3.1
Religion	3.1
Humour	3.0
Monogamy	2.9
Swearing	2.7
Veganism	2.5
Marriage	2.1
Sportiness	1.9
Football	1.7
Tattoos	1.7
Music	1.7

You might wonder if beliefism is associated with any background characteristics. I looked at this by beliefs about the top nine attributes – drug use, trans rights, immigration, inequalities, alcohol, freedom of speech, politics, abortion and the environment – which could all be thought of as 'policy issues' in comparison to the remaining 'personal' ones. There is very little difference by age, gender and ethnicity for any of the issues and no difference by political leaning and education for the personal issues. But Labour voters want to avoid people with different views on the policy issues more than do Conservative voters (an average of 4.8 versus 4.1). Most interestingly perhaps, those with a degree want to avoid people with different policy views more than those without a degree (4.9 versus 4.3). This confirms something that I have long believed and observed: that working-class people are a lot more tolerant than they are sometimes given credit for, and often more tolerant than their middle-class counterparts.

I was going to add to the list whether it matters that a 'scone' is called a 'scon' by some people. It clearly does matter, as it's obviously called a scone, rhyming with 'bone'. I know that posh people, Scottish folk and northerners call it a scon rhyming with 'gone' but they clearly can't talk proper. But it's not on the list because it is a very British debate. Nonetheless, I do feel like I should at least make those of you who are unfamiliar with a cream tea aware of the delight of a cup of tea (English Breakfast, of course) and a scone slathered with clotted cream and jam. Please note here that the cream *must* go on the scone first and then the jam and *not* the other way round. This is non-negotiable, and it's entirely legitimate to discriminate against someone who would put the jam on first.

I digress. None of us can completely free ourselves of beliefism. Moreover, we might not always want to. In fact, I wonder whether some of your more beliefist responses above fill you with pride at your integrity? As noted above, some beliefism might be a good thing, such as when we are intolerant of racists and, as always, we must be alert to context. Moreover, while most people will not admit to being racist or sexist, to be beliefist carries much less opprobrium. Indeed, some people will wear their dogma as a badge of honour, and dismissing some people and their views is often seen as a sign of strength. This makes beliefism different and more complicated than the other isms. Not only will there be conditions under which *some* beliefism will be better than none but also conditions under which people might wish actively to signal their beliefism to curry favour.

My own average on the 'avoid questions' was 2.0, putting me in the lowest quartile of the 'Fab 500'. As someone who has a tattooed sleeve and swears a fair bit, I had tattoos and swearing above several of the policy ones. Those who hate tattoos and swearing would want to avoid me a lot more, I reckon, and so I feel somewhat justified in being beliefist towards them. One thing's for sure, I really don't like being around snobs. I also struggle spending time around people who take themselves very seriously, and I have been beliefist towards them in the past. Since I've started writing about beliefism, though, I feel compelled to at least *try* to practise what I preach. There are plenty of snobbish and overly serious people out there, and I'm *trying* not to dismiss everything they have to say. While some people are best kept at arm's length, I'm *trying* to remind myself that no one, bar the most hostile people in society, should be out of reach. It's fucking hard, though.

Before we move on, I reckon it might be worth doing a quick 'beliefism audit' of your own friendship group so you can get some sense of how aligned your friends' beliefs are with your own. How many of the issues above do you know their beliefs about? How many are like yours? How cognitively diverse is your friendship group? How much does any of this really matter to you? Also consider how much your friends judge – or avoid or are hostile towards – those who have different beliefs to them on these issues. Do you or they have any 'red lines' that would prevent you or them being friends with someone no matter what other qualities they possessed? Regardless of how you answer those questions, I hope that you're convinced of the merits of less beliefism and are willing to join me in my ambition for a more tolerant world.

A duck and a rabbit walk into a bar

Beliefism is predicated on our propensity to take sides, and to split ideas and other people into 'right' and 'wrong', 'good' and 'bad'. Take a look at the image below. What do you see? A duck? A rabbit? It is in fact an illusion that contains the images of both a duck *and* a rabbit. According to Wikipedia, which we all know is the fount of all knowledge, it has its origins in a German humour magazine, with a caption saying something along the lines that the duck and the rabbit would be the two animals most likely to notice one another.[5] Aside from the insights this provides about what Germans find funny, the duck–rabbit illusion is a great way to describe some of the mechanisms through which we take sides on a range of subjects. The image below is taken from my London School of Economics (LSE) 'duck–rabbit' podcast, which discussed issues that polarise us and, in many ways, acted as a catalyst for this book.

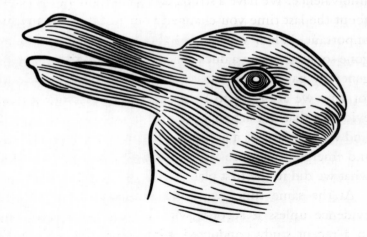

When you first look at the illusion, you will see only one of the animals. Most people will need to be told that there is another animal in the image. Even when they are told it's there, it can be hard for them to recognise the second animal. And when they *do* notice, it remains easier to revert to seeing the first animal again. Both animals are always present, and yet none of us can see the image as both animals simultaneously. It is effortful to keep reminding ourselves, let alone anyone else, that two animals are in the image. Our brains prefer a simple life. We quickly come to see an issue either as a duck or as a rabbit. Once we see it as such, we have no real incentive to see it for the complexity the issue is sure to contain. It's just too effortful to weigh up all the pros and cons of which toothpaste to choose, let alone which party to vote for or person to like.

We pick a side and stick with it. Quite quickly, we can become entrenched in our view and become unwilling to accept that there might be another way of thinking about the issue. There is much more comfort in the simplicity of it being a duck *or* a rabbit rather than in the complexities of ambivalence. We have a strong distaste for ambiguity. Think about the last time you changed your mind about anything important. When was it, and about what? Have you ever gone so far as seeing a duck when you once saw a rabbit? We generally pay attention to evidence and other justifications for why we are right to believe as we do. If we encounter evidence that doesn't support our beliefs, we will typically find ways to dismiss it as lacking in robustness and relevance, and emerge even more assured that we were right to believe what we did in the first place.

At the same time, we are becoming less accepting of evidence unless it accords with what we already believe. In a recent study conducted with colleagues, I show that individuals express greater support for stringent restrictions during Covid in perpetuity when they believe that scientists are the source of moral guidance.[6] Importantly, however, we also drew distinctions between belief in science that is 'well-placed' and that which is 'misplaced'. While the distinction is clearly very blurred and admittedly imperfect, well-placed beliefs included items such as 'Covid vaccines are effective at reducing hospital admissions and deaths from Covid', and misplaced beliefs in science included statements such as 'in case of community outbreaks, outdoor spaces (beaches, parks) should be closed'. Those in favour of restrictions become even more supportive of lockdowns irrespective of whether the scientific evidence was well-placed or misplaced.

There is now neuroscientific evidence to suggest that each belief is maintained by a network of neurons that strengthen through recurrent connections, amplifying the belief through excitatory feedback.[7] This neural activity suggests that beliefs can be resistant to change even when faced with evidence to the contrary. Little wonder, then, that most of us fail to update what we think when fresh evidence becomes available and carry on believing what we thought in the first place. Tipping points represent thresholds of accumulated evidence required to shift a belief from one stable state to another – but it takes a lot to tip. And we do all of this despite our beliefs and world views often being based on very limited information and shaped by subtle and sometimes spurious factors, just as the animal you see first will depend on whether it's around Eastertime, in which case you're more likely to see the rabbit first.[8]

We have an incentive to commit to our beliefs once we have publicly declared them in the same way as we are more likely to lose weight when we publicly commit to doing so.[9] We value consistency. I admit to making some public judgements (based on solid evidence, obviously . . .) that would be hard to change even if there was robust evidence to suggest

I should. I think that the benefits of mindfulness training have been greatly exaggerated and that no one *really* likes spending time with kids under the age of three. My desire for consistency means that I am psychologically motivated to come up with holes in any evidence supporting the claims that mindfulness can help anyone, and that the presence of young kids is a genuine source of happiness. This process of *motivated reasoning* to dismiss evidence at odds with our belief will only serve to further strengthen our faith in it.[10] We were smart to pick the right side in the first place and even smarter now that we have managed to resolve any ambivalence about the 'rightness' of what we believe to be true.

To be clear, though, this is not a book about how to get you to see a rabbit when you are convinced you see a duck. I'm not looking for you to change your beliefs. Rather, my focus is on how we can all learn to accept – and even EMBRACE – that others may quite legitimately see a rabbit when we see a duck. I've not used, and capitalised, the word 'embrace' by accident here. As we will see later, the letters of embrace form my memorable and hopeful impactful mnemonic for effective interventions to facilitate increased tolerance of different beliefs – and in ways that go beyond simply willing ourselves to be less beliefist. We're all guilty of being intolerant from time to time, and despite generally seeing ourselves as tolerant. So, this is a book for everyone who is both somewhat beliefist and a tad deluded about just how tolerant they are. A book for everyone, then.

My first intellectual hero in the early 1990s was Professor Alan Williams at the University of York. His office door had a sign on it which read 'Be reasonable. Do it my way'. He called a duck a duck, but I also witnessed him change his mind when better arguments were presented. I was very proud of an acknowledgement he made to me in one of his key papers, thanking me for helping to shape his views in my 'characteristically argumentative way'.[11] Since you are reading this book, I know that you're more likely to be on the tolerant end of the spectrum already, so perhaps the challenge for you is how to help those less tolerant folk around you to become more so. I'm sure Alan helped to make me more tolerant. Most things in life are contagious, remember. Misery certainly is. There's no reason to suppose that beliefism is any different. So don't underestimate your power to influence those around you.

You could see this as a book designed to take the heat out of *how we relate* to one another rather than out of *how we debate* one another. Insofar as I chose to be an academic, I did so because I wanted to be able to research topics that interest me, to become better informed, and perhaps even to change my mind about what I thought to be true from time to time. Most of all, I wanted to debate ideas. I have always loved a good argument, and I still enjoy hearing a range of views, especially on topics that I know relatively little about. My vision is a world where those who see ducks and those who see rabbits are just as likely to be friends as foes – and even have a drink together.

Splitting image

I'm proud to have friends from different social classes and from across the political spectrum with whom to discuss a variety of issues. One of my mates is Steve Baker, who was the Conservative MP for Wycombe until July 2024 when he lost his seat in the general election. We met during the pandemic, when we were both convinced that several of the social distancing policy responses to Covid in the UK would cause more harm than good. I don't agree with him about everything and we have very different views about economic issues (he's much more trusting of the market than I am and I'd like to see much more redistribution than he would). But we would be friends even if we also disagreed about the policy responses to the pandemic, although we would have been unlikely to have met. The answer to why I like Steve is a simple one: I like him. He is a principled man, and these principles extend to respecting different opinions. He is kind and generous – including towards those who disagree with him.

It's hardly the most insightful thing in the world to say that I'm friends with people I like, and they need to like me too, of course. But here's the thing: they don't have to *be* like me. My friends don't have to share the same beliefs as me. Some of them are quite like me but many of them have very different beliefs and my friendship group contains people who voted for every one of the main political parties at the 2024 election in the UK. I enjoy discussing topics with every one of them and get great pleasure and purpose from arguing with those that I disagree with – and sometimes even more so than from discussions with people who think similarly to me. Alongside my distaste for snobbery and seriousness, I have a very low tolerance of sanctimony. I appreciate I'm dangerously close to that line in writing this (or I might have crossed it). But I am proud of having a diverse group of mates, both in backgrounds and beliefs. I try very hard to avoid seeing someone as all good or all bad based on their beliefs – well, apart from sanctimonious snobs who take themselves seriously, of course.

To see someone in black and white terms is what some psychotherapists refer to as *splitting*. (It's probably worth confessing at this point that my wife is a psychotherapist who uses that term a fair bit.) Children will often ask whether someone is good or bad. Our kids did it a lot when they were younger and our response was always the same: all of us are simultaneously amazing and awful. It's not only kids who are guilty of splitting. I mention Steve Baker here because he was one of the main architects of Brexit. A few Remainer colleagues at the LSE, where finding someone who publicly supported Brexit really is about as likely as finding rocking-horse shit, have asked me how I can be friends with Brexiteer Steve. Their assumption that I am also an ardent Remainer is very presumptuous, of course, and is indicative of their belief that they were 'right' while anyone who wanted the UK to control more of its laws was 'wrong'. (My own view on Brexit, for what it's worth now, was that we should have voted to Remain, but I didn't feel especially strongly about the issue.)

Splitting is explained in large part by the *fundamental attribution error* (FAE).[12] The FAE is a pervasive psychological phenomenon whereby we overemphasise personality-based explanations for behaviours observed in others while overemphasising situational explanations for ourselves. This means that we attribute morally questionable actions to another person's character while at the same time explaining our own behaviour away by recourse to the specific context of our actions. So, if you were to observe someone else stealing a bar of chocolate, you would be likely to consider them to be a thief. But if you stole a bar of chocolate, I bet you wouldn't see yourself as a thief but rather as someone whose actions were justified in that set of circumstances: maybe you had lost your payment card, or you'd overpaid by mistake before.

It's so much easier for us to categorise other people as either good or bad rather than go to the effort of judging them on each issue. Once an ardent Remainer views someone as a nasty Brexiteer, or vice versa, they might always view that person as nasty. Many of my colleagues at LSE seemingly hate Steve's views about Brexit, and therefore they simply hate him. They can't see past his views on one issue to even contemplate that they might agree with him on other issues, let alone to allow themselves to give a moment's thought to the fact that he might be a decent bloke. These are highly educated people with PhDs at a minimum. Formal education is no antidote to the FAE.

When it comes to friendships, I would like to think that kindness, generosity, humour and other important qualities should matter more than politics when we're deciding whether to be friends with someone. But Pew Research Center data from 2019 indicates a significant divide in social circles based on political affiliations in the US, with 66 per cent of Democrats and 55 per cent of Republicans reporting few to no close friends from the opposing party.[13] Party affiliation in the US is heavily tied to race and religion, making intergroup contact even less likely. A study from 2016 in the US found that residing in an area with opposing political views makes it more difficult for people to form friendships.[14] These and other data from the US point to a deepening of *partisan sorting* in personal relationships. Similar patterns are observed in the UK[15] and Europe but to nowhere near the same extent. As with many issues relating to partisan politics, we must be alert not to extrapolate too much from the US.

Interestingly, recent evidence from various countries, including the UK and Germany as well as the US, suggests that women have been moving leftward politically, while men are tending more towards the right.[16] This divergence in political opinions between the sexes has been attributed to several factors, including education, economic and cultural frustrations, and less mixed socialising. If liberal women are increasingly avoiding conservative men in dating markets, this will lead to increased partisan sorting. In an online dating experiment with 3,000 adults in the UK, we looked at the degree to which people want to date someone who votes for the same party (Conservative or Labour) alongside other characteristics, such as facial attractiveness.[17] It turns out that partisanship matters almost as much as attractiveness. And it matters more to women who vote Labour than it does to any other categorisation of gender and party affiliation.

We also found that one of the key aspects of dating decisions is whether the other person signals in their profile that they are tolerant of other world views. This is true even for individuals that self-identify as intolerant. No one likes intolerant people, not even those of us who are intolerant. So, if you're on a dating site right now, I suggest you try and signal your open-mindedness (and even more so if you actually *are* open-minded). In one way or another, we are all trying to convince ourselves and other people that we are a 'good' person. People with 'good' reputations benefit in all sorts of ways, from more choice in dating and labour markets, to generally being happier. While there is nothing wrong with wanting a partner whose values are aligned with yours, it is possible that what really matters to a relationship's success – such as kindness, generosity and humour – might not have as much to do with political preferences as people might imagine.

Whatever the precise details on partisan sorting, I'm very curious to understand why so many people appear to be more beliefist than I consider myself to be. Are their beliefs stronger than mine? Or maybe they're more fragile? Am I more tolerant than them? Or maybe less principled? I could be deluded about my own degree of tolerance. I might also be trying to signal it to you. I have previously written about how when someone says something about themselves it is often to convince others, and sometimes themselves, that they are someone they are not. Kind people rarely tell you how kind they are. Truly busy people don't have the time to. But I have always admired people who are different: those who look different, and act, and think differently. And sometimes just because they are different. I'm a big fan of protestors. I admire people who glue their hands to the pavement. I rarely agree with their cause, and I frequently consider their tactics to be self-defeating. But I love that they care. I admire their passion.

Well-functioning societies require a distribution of people and beliefs, remember. This is an important point to keep in mind throughout. I have been impacted greatly by the wisdom of crowds.[18] The basic idea comes from estimates of the weight of an ox. People walk past it and guess what it weighs – independently of one another. Some people give crazy estimates, but the mean is remarkably accurate. Challenges such as the future of AI are a long way from the weight of an ox, but it might turn out that the beliefs of many people are a more accurate representation of what will come to pass than relying on a handful of experts (who also disagree wildly with one another). A distribution of beliefs should go hand in hand with less beliefism. If we can nudge a significant number of people towards slightly less beliefism, we will create a better society with better decision making at all levels. From this, we can expect more interaction, cooperation, and genuine friendships, between people with different perspectives. So, no boring consensus, then, but rather robust and respectful argument.

The spillover effects of beliefism

Reducing beliefism is not going to be easy. Once we know – or think we know – what someone believes, it will often affect how we behave towards them, and sometimes in ways in which we might be unaware. The distinction between *knowing* and *thinking that we know* someone's beliefs will be a substantive one on some occasions, but most of the time it won't make much difference to how we treat them. If I am strongly pro-choice on abortion, say, and beliefist, and I have some reason to *believe* that you are strongly pro-life, then I may discriminate against you in a host of ways. That reason could be anything from seeing you at a pro-life rally to being told you are pro-life by someone whom I trust. As with so much in life, it's our perceptions that determine so much of what we think, do and feel. Whether we are aware or unaware of our discrimination may not make much difference to how we treat people either, though the effects in the latter case will likely be more subtle.

Imagine that the (presumed to be) pro-lifer is a work colleague. In principle, I ought to be able to put my aversive reaction to their views on abortion to one side when we're discussing another issue. But if I can't (consciously or unconsciously) ignore their beliefs about abortion, then I might dismiss their beliefs about other things. I might even look less favourably on their views about how productivity could be improved. Equally, I might find out that my colleague shares the same views on abortion as me, and then I find myself (consciously and unconsciously) agreeing with them, including about how to improve productivity. It's hard to think of any good reasons why someone's beliefs about abortion should affect the quality of their beliefs about how to get more output from a given input in the workplace. Beliefism can therefore result in considerable *spillover effects* when we allow our judgements of someone's beliefs on one topic or domain to determine our judgements of their beliefs, views or preferences on domains that we ought to be forming separate judgements about.

Together with my friends and colleagues Matteo Galizzi and Dario Krpan, I have conducted research on behavioural spillovers and 'spillunders' – on how one behaviour affects the next and how the intention to do something later affects what you do before that.[19] Dropping a pebble of change into the behavioural pond will not only cause an initial splash but it will have significant behavioural ripple effects downstream, and sometimes upstream. Going to the gym now or deciding to go later, for example, has a significant effect on food choices before and afterwards – sometimes in ways that reinforce being healthy, sometimes in ways that sabotage being healthy. This is an example of a within-domain spillover – in this case, health. There can also be across-domain spillovers, such as when my levels of physical activity (or more accurately, how I feel about my activity levels) impact upon how much I give to charity. No behaviour – or belief – sits in a vacuum.

Some beliefs that we hold will be correlated with one another, and so it's not unreasonable to sometimes use one belief to predict another. There is some evidence, mostly from the US, to suggest that beliefs have become more 'clustered' over time. In other words, once I know your views about freedom of speech, I am now better able to predict your views on immigration and climate change than I was a couple of decades ago.[20] Using a basket of ten political attitude measures, including views about immigration and the environment, Pew Research data from the US show that the median (middle) Republican is now more conservative than 94 per cent of Democrats, and the middle Democrat is more liberal than 92 per cent of Republicans. These percentages were around 70 per cent and 64 per cent respectively in 1994.[21]

In a 2022 paper, George Melios and colleagues have showed that such ideological consistency has further spillover implications for policy. Looking at beliefs about what is the role of government and how competent different parties are causally affects the overall amount partisans donate to charities. Using seventeen years of US tax return data, the paper shows that when individuals support the current government, they tend to reduce their charitable contributions and, when they oppose the government, they increase their donations. While these differences are likely to be explained by perceptions of the effectiveness of government, those perceptions will be to some considerable degree influenced by partisan preferences and the degree of beliefism.[22]

Further, recent studies with longitudinal data have shown, remarkably, that these conditions are leading some Americans to adjust their demographic identities to better align with partisan and ideological prototypes. Using nationally representative surveys of the adult US population, and questions about a range of identities, researchers found that in 2006–14 substantial numbers of Americans shifted in and out of identities associated with ethnicity, religion, sexual orientation and class.[23] A small but significant share of people shifted their identities in ways that conform with political group prototypes. Liberal Democrats were more likely than conservative Republicans to shift into identification as lesbian, gay or bisexual; having no religion; and being of Latino origin; and conservative Republicans were more likely than liberal Democrats to shift into identification as born-again Christian and Protestant.

The patterns of clustering found in the US do not seem to be repeated quite so much in the UK. Indeed, if anything, people are becoming less committed to one party over time (and have clustered more around Brexit than party affiliation[24]). I'm editing this paragraph a few days after Labour won a landslide at the 2024 general election. Many voters shifted from the Tories to the Lib Dems and to Reform. Despite its landslide in Parliament, where they won 63 per cent of the seats, Labour's share of the vote rose only slightly to 34 per cent. The turnout was 60 per cent, the lowest since 2001. Overall, the vote reflected a rejection of the Conservative government much more than an overwhelming endorsement of Labour, but it did highlight that people can move around with their vote to some extent. Above all, though, the election highlighted the vagaries of the first-past-the-post voting system: Labour needed around 24,000 votes for each seat won compared to 800,000 for Reform. Any reasonable democrat should surely prefer a more proportional system.

In any case, even if it's now easier to identify groups of people with similar beliefs across a range of issues than it once was, the correlations remain far from perfect. And even if they are higher than they once were, it remains problematic to take people's views on one set of beliefs and use those to judge and discriminate against them in wholly unrelated contexts. And yet the spillover effects of beliefism have been found to be pervasive. Imagine you needed a plumber and had two to choose from: one who was a great plumber but broke off associations with friends and contractors of a certain race; and another who was just a decent plumber but didn't discriminate in that way. Which would you choose? What if the second plumber was crap at their job, and you had to pick one or the other? How easy is it for you to decide? Most forms of beliefism spillovers relate to contexts that are much more benign than racist behaviour but no less impactful on important outcomes that we care about such as productivity and social justice.

A set of interesting studies conducted in 2019 looked at whether the tendency to prefer advice from politically like-minded people generalises to domains that have nothing to do with politics. Participants had multiple opportunities to learn about other people's political opinions and their ability to categorise geometric shapes. When confronted with categorising shapes, even simple ones, participants had to decide who to turn to for advice. Political allegiance shouldn't play any role here as it was uncorrelated with the ability to categorise shapes. The results, based on data from 340 people, showed something quite different: participants falsely concluded that people who think the same way as they do politically were better at categorising shapes, and so they leaned more heavily on partisans for advice.[25]

Recent research has explored the influence of beliefism spillovers on various aspects of economic behaviour. One study conducted a series of experiments 'in the field' with Ghanaian taxi drivers around the 2008 elections.[26] The study used fare bargaining in Ghana's ethnically diverse capital city, Accra. Passengers hail a taxi, and the fare negotiation takes place outside the vehicle until a fare is agreed. Flyers encouraging participation in the study were distributed around one of the biggest transportation hubs in Accra. The rider was asked to hail a cab and relay an opening script in his ethnic mother tongue to begin the negotiation. The rider and driver learn one another's ethnicity through language and accent, and infer partisanship based on the typical nesting of ethnic groups in parties, just as they would in everyday life. The results showed that the cabbies were inclined to accept lower fares from passengers who shared their political affiliation while demanding higher prices from those who supported opposing parties.

In a study conducted in the US in 2016, around 1,800 people received an email with an offer to register their interest for purchasing a discounted Amazon gift card.[27] The card was worth $50, and participants would be asked to pay only $25 if they were selected to buy the card. All subjects were told in the email that the cards were leftover thank-you gifts for volunteers who had raised money. The offer was the same, but the text of the email was different across three randomly assigned groups. The first group was told that the gift cards were left over from 'our collaboration with volunteers on Democratic campaigns'. The second group was told that the collaboration was with volunteers on Republican campaigns. The third (control) group was told that the cards were left over from work with a nonprofit organisation. Participants indicated their interest by clicking on a link and completing a survey that asked them to affirm their desire to purchase the card. Participants were nearly twice as likely to respond to the emails when they shared partisan affiliation with the fundraiser.

Beliefism may sometimes be justified, such as when we turn away from the abhorrent views of an intransigent person, and sometimes we may be right to ignore all the views of a beliefist person simply by virtue of their beliefism getting in the way of good judgement. But by and large, beliefism spillovers will typically get in the way of effective decision making. You may not wish to engage with a religious person who wants to limit your rights to an abortion or to drink alcohol on a Sunday and who is unwilling to debate you on these issues. But this does not mean that you should ignore their beliefs on other issues they are willing to discuss with you. This certainly does not mean that you should disregard their views on how to improve workplace performance, for example. We would be throwing the belief baby out with the beliefism bathwater if we ignored all the beliefs of a beliefist.

2

When two tribes go to war

Birds of a feather

Beliefism and its various spillover effects are predicated on us seeing someone else as different to us. And how we see ourselves will be determined by how we view the groups to which we belong. All academic disciplines as well as common sense recognise that we are social animals. We have evolved to be part of a group, and to belong. We use others as the standard against which to compare ourselves, and we seek to fit in. The area with possibly the largest body of academic work in the behavioural sciences is social norms, where we take on the beliefs and behaviours of those around us. Imagine walking down a street and seeing loads of people looking up. What do you do? Look up, almost certainly. Imagine having an overdue tax bill and finding out that 95 per cent of people in your local area pay their taxes on time? What do you do? File your tax return, probably. Imagine coming to believe that all your friends exercise more than you? What do you do? Exercise more, possibly.[28]

There are three pathways through which we take on the behaviour and identity of the group to which we belong. First, social influence, whereby we conform to group norms because of peer pressure and authority influence. Think of how the culture of your workplace is determined. Second, shared experiences, ranging from historical events to common struggles or achievements. Think of the solidarity of the Windrush generation in the UK. Third, cultural transmission, whereby traditions are passed down from one generation to the next through folklore, rituals and education. Think of how West Ham fans will never forget that we won the World Cup for England in 1966 (the captain and both goal scorers played for the Hammers at that time).

We also like people more when they resemble us in various ways, including how they view the world. When we see the image as a duck, we surround ourselves with others who see a duck too: 'birds of a feather flock together'. This is referred to as *homophily*.[29] We are more likely to have friends who have similar characteristics to us, even if sometimes we are unaware of surrounding ourselves with people like us. This phenomenon isn't limited to mere friendship circles; it permeates every aspect of our social lives including work relationships and the networks we build for support and advice. Indeed, our social circles are astonishingly uniform, primarily segregated by age, race and education. Intriguingly, relationships between dissimilar individuals are more prone to dissolve, paving the way for even tighter-knit clusters within our social spaces.[30]

Groups of like-minded people can be very effective, of course. And sometimes dissenting voices can get in the way of effective decision making (as well as being bloody

annoying). Several theories and models elucidate the mechanisms driving the ways that groups think. A prominent
theory here is *transactive memory system* (TMS), which posits
that, in cohesive groups, members assume specialised roles.[31]
Each team member relies on the specialised knowledge of
their colleagues and the whole is greater than the sum of its
parts. Unsurprisingly, communication plays a pivotal role in
group cognition. Through open dialogue, group members
exchange ideas, negotiate and amalgamate their individual
viewpoints. This culminates in a collective understanding or
solution that might have been elusive on an individual level.
This is how communication and collaboration in the most
effective households, clubs and workplaces operate.

Not all groups make effective decisions, though, and group
cognition can be undermined in several ways. Dominant
personalities can unintentionally or intentionally suppress
the voices and ideas of others, for example, which leads to a
narrowed viewpoint. Perhaps the most noteworthy negative
consequence of group cognition is *groupthink*.[32] This is where
a group of individuals reaches and reinforces a consensus
without a proper evaluation of the alternatives. The quest
for harmony in a group can impede its cognitive processes
and can culminate in suboptimal decision making if better
choices are ruled out too quickly because of the urge to reach
agreement. At its core, groupthink stems from a collective
desire to maintain harmony and avoid conflict. We all have
a deep-seated desire to fit in – even those, and sometimes
especially those, who profess how much they seek to stand
out.[33] We care about what other group members think about
us. A lot.

Groupthink and beliefism are inextricably linked. Within
a group experiencing groupthink, individual members
often feel a strong pressure to align their opinions with the

perceived group consensus. This pressure can come from a genuine desire to maintain group harmony or from fear of being ostracised. Groupthink can create a false sense of agreement. Even if only a few members vocalise their agreement, it may be perceived as if everyone agrees, especially if dissenting voices remain silent. In groups dominated by groupthink, alternative viewpoints or criticisms are often suppressed, either actively by group leaders or passively by group members themselves who self-censor out of fear of going against the grain. The group may isolate themselves from outside opinions, believing that their decisions are superior or that outsiders wouldn't understand. And so the group becomes ever more certain that the world is precisely – and only – as they see it.

Even if someone disagrees with the views of the group, it is very hard for them to speak out. I can't emphasise enough how much we want to fit in – even when we know *for sure* that fitting in will lead to the wrong decision.[34] Groupthink is compounded by *availability cascades*. These are self-reinforcing processes of collective belief formation, which can increase beliefism by entrenching extreme viewpoints within a community or society.[35] When certain narratives or pieces of information become more prominent and widely shared, often through media and social networks, they can create a feedback loop where the perceived prevalence of these views leads to their increased acceptance by the group. This can reduce openness to alternative perspectives.

Consider economic forecasting.[36] Imagine a group of experts predict that inflation in the next period will be 5 per cent and that one expert believes it will be somewhat lower. That expert faces a choice between fitting in or sticking their neck out with a lower forecast. If they do the latter and are right, then great, but if they are wrong, they will feel like an idiot. It is much better for their happiness and ego to fit in, even if that means they all end up being wrong, rather than to stand out and possibly end up as the *only one* who is wrong. This is one possible explanation for why economic forecasts are frequently wrong and, in the words of J. K. Galbraith, 'make astrology look respectable'.[37] The point here is that our desires to fit in can often be so strong as to trump any desire to be 'right'.

Feeling beliefist

The beliefs of a group affect not only how that group behaves and feels about itself – the in-group – but also how it acts towards and feels about another group – the out-group. On top of splitting people into good and bad, we will often split the world into 'us' and 'them'. This has deep philosophical roots in *moral dualism*, which guides us to categorise the world into dichotomies of good and bad, virtuous and evil. Throughout history, narratives have been created about the benevolence of the in-group and the malevolence of the out-group. As we worry about the recent impact of social media, it is sometimes easy to forget that we have long sought to ascribe moral superiority to the in-group and, at the same time, to demonise the out-group. When we feel that our group or the identity that we associate with it is under threat, we will often react by digging our heels into our own group and kicking out against the out-group.

The differences between groups can be magnified by misguided *meta-perceptions*. These are our beliefs about how our own in-group is perceived by the out-group. Frequently, we will carry around beliefs of how others see us that have very little to do with how they really see us. Erroneous beliefs often stem from stereotyping and prejudice, and we over-estimate the extent to which the other group holds negative beliefs about our group. This exaggeration fosters further hostility between groups. The duck and the rabbit might not actually be that far apart from one another, though they might be from time to time, but, either way, *belief traps* magnify mistaken perceptions about out-groups, further fuelling beliefism.[38] And quickly battle lines are drawn between ducks and rabbits, as beautifully represented below.

"There can be no peace until they renounce their Rabbit God and accept our Duck God."

Consider a recent survey of over 1,000 American adults.[39] Participants identifying as either Democrats or Republicans were asked to rate their feelings towards the opposite party. Participants were asked to rate partisans in terms of honesty and intelligence when compared to other Americans on a five-point scale. In 2022, around two-thirds of Democrats thought that Republicans were more dishonest than other Americans and about three-quarters of Republicans thought that Democrats were more dishonest. For both parties, about one-half of people thought that supporters of the other party were less intelligent than other Americans. Perhaps no surprises here, but the proportions were up from less than a half on honesty and less than a third on intelligence from only six years earlier.

For some UK evidence on misperceptions of beliefs, in a recent study from colleagues at the LSE, 3,326 participants in the UK were asked how well they thought some characteristics described the two sides of the main political parties on a scale from 1 ('not at all well') to 5 ('very well'). For perceptions of honesty, Labour respondents rated their own side 3.8 and Conservative supporters at 2.5, whereas Conservative respondents rated their own side 3.5 and Labour supporters at 2.1. Regarding Brexit identities, both Leavers and Remainers rated their own side at 4.0 and the other side as 3.0. For perceptions of closed-mindedness, Labour respondents rated their own side at 2.6 and Conservatives at 3.8. Conservative supporters rated their own side at 2.2 and Labour supporters at 3.7. Leavers rated other Leavers at 2 and Remainers at 3.7. Remainers rated other Remainers at 1.9 and Leavers at 3.4. In a nutshell, the out-group is seen as less honest and a whole lot less open-minded.

The clear delineation of groups lends itself to *affective polarisation* (AP). It is typically measured by taking the difference between positive feelings towards the in-group and negative feelings towards the out-group. While the differences between groups in beliefs hasn't increased too much in recent years, several studies have shown that how the groups *feel* about one another has become more polarised.[40] The figure opposite shows AP in the UK, US, Germany and Sweden between 1977 and 2020. It uses a 'feeling thermometer' to measure feelings, with ratings from 0 (unfavourably) to 100 (favourably). People consistently feel quite positively about their own political party but feelings towards the opposing party have become increasingly negative over time. For the UK, it's interesting to observe that the country was becoming less polarised until the Brexit referendum but has become much more so since. Germany and Sweden show different patterns with a general 'de-polarising' trend. There is some suggestive evidence that this might be related to the rise of coalition governments in these countries.[41]

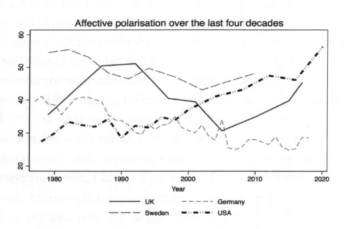

Affective polarisation over the last four decades

Note: The numbers show average differences of liking own political party and main rival on a 0-100 scale

Evidence from the US suggests that people tend to become more polarised as they get older. This is partly because, as people age, their loyalty to their own party strengthens. Additionally, each new generation is starting off slightly more polarised than the previous one, entering adulthood with stronger party biases.[42] While age-based polarisation is evident in the US, Europe offers a different picture. A study examining ideological positions across twenty-seven

European countries from 1981 to 2018 reveals that polarisation by age has, by and large, remained relatively constant.
Interestingly, the young in Europe simultaneously favour
smaller government and progressive social issues, but the
degree to which they express hostility towards those (older
people) who think differently to them is unclear.

The concept of defining oneself by an 'anti-identity' plays a
significant role in our understanding and analysis of affective
polarisation. You might like to consider for a moment a group
that you really like and one that you really dislike. I suspect
your feelings of hostility towards the latter are much stronger
than your feelings of fondness towards the former. Beyond this,
you might identify yourself as being the kind of person who
is more against an out-group than in favour of an in-group.
Some people may now define themselves as being anti-racist
as opposed to simply being non-racist, for example. There is
arguably a much clearer group identity in fighting the social
injustices of racism compared to being against racial discrimination. Quite what the alternative to anti-racism represents
and whether anti-racism has led to less racism are moot points
here; it's the identity of being explicitly 'anti' that matters.

Evidence suggests that the construction of anti-identities can
sometimes be used by political entities or movements to gal-
vanise support and cement in-group cohesion and out-group
animosity. This is achieved by delineating clear boundaries
between 'us' and 'them', which reduces complex issues to a
demonisation of the out-group. Recent work shows that fund-
raising emails containing negative political identity cues lead to
higher donations than those that tap into positive identity. In an
experiment with a sample of nearly 90,000 people conducted
with a political party (not disclosed) in the UK around the time
of the 2019 election, a single campaign email containing negative comments about the opposing party drove up donations

by 15 per cent compared to not receiving any campaign email at all.[43] This study did not compare activating 'pro' and 'anti' identities, but the results provide fresh empirical evidence on the behavioural effects of activating anti-identities.

Moreover, we can sometimes feel better if we have someone to blame for how bad the world is. By holding the out-group responsible, and by vilifying them, we absolve ourselves of the responsibility of trying to change things. It's them wot ruined it. George Melios has some data suggesting that when people in the UK who care about reducing inequality move into areas of higher inequality, they don't become any more concerned about inequality or more actively involved in reducing it. Instead, they become more hostile towards the Conservatives, presumably because they hold them responsible for inequality. Whether the Tories are responsible for inequality is not important here. It is easier and feels better to hold them responsible, and it's a whole lot easier than actually doing something about it.

Taking the path of least resistance is a generalisable and substantively rational response to changed circumstances. David Bradford and I have developed a theoretical model, showing that, when people gain weight, they can maintain their happiness levels by either losing weight or adjusting how much their weight matters to their overall happiness.[44] The latter is easier than the former and this is exactly what we find people doing in empirical analysis designed to test our model. It's not that caring less about your weight is straightforward, it's just relatively easier than losing weight, which is notoriously hard and something that about 99 per cent of obese people fail to do into the longer term. In a related way, wherever blame and hostility are easier responses to maintain happiness levels than acting, we should expect to find an increase in affective polarisation and beliefism.

It is worth noting here that AP can sometimes be a good thing. It can serve as a catalyst for engaging those typically disinterested in politics, thus resulting in higher voter turnout when oppositional feelings towards political adversaries intensify. AP may facilitate the decentralisation of power, bolster collective decision-making accuracy, and amplify the voices of politically underrepresented individuals.[45] In a heterogeneous society, political identities will inevitably vary, and AP can be seen as reflecting the degree to which various groups have succeeded in projecting their preferred positions into the public discourse. Rather than forcing uniformity, AP can signify an endeavour towards the coexistence of diverse identities. We must always be alert to context but, overall, AP serves to widen divisions in society not because of the polarisation – difference and extremes are healthy – but because of the affective part – hostile feelings towards others are largely harmful.

I should now distinguish affective polarisation from my conceptualisation of beliefism. AP refers to the phenomenon where members of different groups feel hostility towards one another. Beliefism is active discrimination against those with different beliefs. Ultimately, AP is all about feelings, although political scientists do take those feelings to manifest as behaviours relating inter alia to voting, activism and social interactions. Beliefism can contain cognitive as well as affective rationalisations, as well as reactions to other people's beliefs. AP is typically used in the context of political parties and ideological tribes. Beliefism refers to discrimination pertaining to any belief, including those relating to personal choices, such as whether to have children or to eat meat. AP is therefore nested within beliefism both in terms of processing in the brain and the object of that processing.

Please also keep in mind that we are interested in the

spillovers of beliefism in this book and not just in beliefism itself. None of us will be immune to allowing how we feel about one belief that someone holds to spill over to how we feel about other beliefs they hold and about them in general. Since it is much easier for us to split on someone or a group – to decide that they are either all good or all bad – we take their views on a single issue as a 'thin slice' of their whole character, and this spills over into how we treat that person or group in general. Being hostile towards me as a West Ham fan is one thing; dismissing my beliefs about how to be happy because I'm a West Ham fan is another thing entirely.

This is the modern world

We have a natural tendency for *rosy retrospection*: to recall the past more favourably than the present.[46] But we have always taken sides, and often with considerable hostility. I was sixteen years old when the miners' strike started in 1984. It remains one of the most divisive issues in the UK of the last fifty years.[47] It was a confrontation born out of animosity between unionised labour and the Conservative government; out of a mutual loathing between Arthur Scargill, president of the National Union of Mineworkers, and Margaret Thatcher, prime minister. It pitted (see what I did there . . .) striking miners against those who returned to work. It pitted miners against the police. Some of the hostilities between these groups remain to this day. The strike lasted a year and involved some violent battles on the picket lines. But, for all the battle lines, it was a confrontation limited to the 'real world'.

Before I get into how the 'virtual world' has exacerbated the 'duck–rabbit problem', it is worth saying that the digital age has broadened our social and intellectual horizons in unimaginably positive ways. OK, now that's out of the way . . . in the modern world of online interactions, we can wade into an issue without too much effort, and with almost unfettered hostility. Social media platforms also make it easier for us to find and engage with information that supports our preconceived ideas, further entrenching us into a 'one animal' view of the world. In a recent study with LSE colleagues, we ran an experiment on 450 US adults to see how they processed information about abortions following the overturning of *Roe v. Wade* in 2022.[48] We found that most people stick with their original beliefs about abortion irrespective of the new information presented to them. We show that this is driven by people actively trying to avoid counter-information rather than by actively seeking confirmatory information.

Social media has also amplified the visibility of *performative activism*, whereby individuals or groups engage in exaggerated expressions of their beliefs.[49] I'm sure you can think of examples of where you sense that someone's extreme views are not necessarily born out of a deep-seated belief in a particular position but rather as a strategy to gain social capital with online communities. Through their algorithmic structures, online platforms encourage and incentivise more extreme and polarised content. The more sensational the content, the greater the attention received. The concept of filter bubbles, or echo chambers, has also been identified as a significant factor contributing to performative extremity online.[50] These are where users are predominantly exposed to information that reinforces their existing beliefs.

In many ways, online behaviours will mimic those in the real world. One of the big differences is that we don't get any feedback about how what we say online about other people impacts upon them. In the real world, we can see people's reactions. When we're hostile or rude or angry, we can see how this upsets them. This feedback helps us to regulate our behaviour (in much the same way, as we shall see in Part 2, that emotional feedback is necessary for effective decision-making). There will be occasions when this constrains us too much in some substantive sense but, by and large, it serves social interactions and general discourse pretty well. Even though some of what people write online about other people is truly awful, there is a general lack of awareness about just how much upset they are causing. This is supported by evidence illustrating the surprise that online trolls have shown when they have heard about how they have affected their victims.[51]

Online behaviours cannot be automatically used to make inferences about offline actions, though. There is perhaps now a significant disconnect between what you would actively like to find out about someone and what you would care about if you were passively or casually to find out. Indeed, there might be things that you would actively like to avoid finding out about. In the modern information age, we can find out much more about each other than we have ever been able to before. On dating sites, for example, we can signal an array of beliefs and preferences about politics, religion, sex and so on before we ever meet anyone. In the past, these were qualities it might take a long time to find out about. I would find out how funny you were a long time before I found out which political party you voted for. Ignorance is bliss, in the sense that I might find out what really matters for our relationship – your kindness, generosity and sense of humour – before finding out about your politics.

This makes me wonder how much of any increase in partisan sorting – and hostility – could be attributable to a 'supply side' effect rather than being demand driven; that is, determined by what people can easily signal about themselves as opposed to that signal being inherently valuable. The signal is almost costless, and it forces the recipient to pay attention to it. It can certainly sometimes feel as if we must have an opinion on everything – and that we must broadcast it to the world. This can then result in people caring about the signal I send about my beliefs not because it is of fundamental value to them but, rather, because its mere presence, at a minimum, forces them to consider its value. Increased partisan identity strengthens the psychological significance of political affiliations, transforming them into mega-identities. This transformation is driven not so much by a genuine belief in the ideologies as by a desire to be part of a group by signalling support and belonging.

There will be plenty of contexts within which signalling strong, and immoveable, views will benefit you. Passionately wading into an issue shows that are a stimulating person and of good character to participate and to care. With reputations visible to the whole world online, we need to make our presence – and sometimes our intransigence – known to everyone. Back in the real world, a football fan isn't going to have many friends if they keep changing allegiances, even among those who support his new team. The first order condition of being a 'proper' football fan is that your team never changes. Under. No. Circumstances. So, if we're going to have any chance of reducing beliefism, we need to consider the incentives, reputational and otherwise, for people to discriminate against people based on their beliefs.

It would be interesting in a future dating experiment to explore how much people would have been willing to pay for information about their prospective date's political views as compared to, say, education level. The former has greater value when all information is costless, but would it still matter more if people had to pay for it? And, more interestingly, might some people be willing to pay to avoid knowing their date's politics? In some of our work on the value of information in relation to calorie labelling, we found that many people are willing to pay not to know calorie information.[52] The context was calorie labelling on popcorn that people were going to consume at the cinema (well, sitting at a computer). We all know popcorn is not the healthiest food around, and so why get reminded of that fact, especially when you're going to eat it anyway? There are surely contexts where 'belief labelling' is just as misery making as calorie labelling. And what a nice segue into discussing the bases of beliefs, which will further inform our discussion of how to reduce beliefism and its harmful effects.

3

You better believe it

Defining beliefs

What beliefs are and where they come from could be a whole book, so forgive me as I race through the issues to retain our focus on beliefism. A belief in this book can be understood as the cognitive acceptance of a proposition, idea or statement as true or real. I can believe all sorts of things about how my life and the world around me *does* look, and about how my life and the world around me *should* look. Some of these beliefs will relate to politics, others to religion, others to economic issues, and others to more personal issues, from views around marriage to whether pizzas should be topped with pineapple. Strongly held beliefs about how the world should be are often referred to as *values*. We will often define ourselves according to our underlying values, which are tied to moral or ethical considerations.

For the purposes of this book, I'm interested in any belief that may result in people being discriminated against for holding it, and so I do not need to distinguish too much between beliefs and values. I'm thankful for this because the boundaries between them can be quite blurred.[53] I noted earlier that beliefism emanates from the *presumption* that another individual or group holds a particular belief with which we disagree. We are frequently mistaken about what other people believe but we typically have some behavioural basis, however spurious or tenuous, upon which to form that judgement – even if that stretches so far as mere hearsay. The substantive point here for beliefism is that you need to know, or be able to assume, something about what I believe that goes beyond the mere presence of a belief inside my head. A racist person needs to observe, or be able to assume, some-thing about someone's race or skin colour for that racism to be activated.

Having been trained as an economist, I think in terms of *preferences*; that is, about the desirability of one alternative over another. Preferences manifest as choices. Fundamentally, there are three kinds of preference: 1) *individual* preferences over our own welfare, e.g., do I buy tea or coffee?; 2) *social* preferences over the welfare of other people when they are considered alongside ourselves, e.g., how much of my income do I keep for myself and how much do I give to family, friends and charity?; and 3) *other-regarding* preferences when we might not be affected by our choice, e.g., do I give to a cancer charity or a donkey sanctuary? We can also have *meta-preferences* over our choices.[54] I might get drunk or lie from time to time, but still have a meta-preference for being sober or being honest. For the sake of simplicity in this book, I will consider meta-preferences to be conceptually synonymous with our values or beliefs about how the world should be.

We might consider cleansing meta-preferences that are 'misguided' or 'pathological'. I've put quotation marks around each of these adjectives because the definition of each is problematic. There is a whole literature in economics and philosophy that discusses the bases upon which preferences should be laundered.[55] It's a moral minefield. Nonetheless, we might all agree that whatever the context of our beliefs, we would require that they are based on legitimate reasons. Put as simply as any of this can be, it would mean that someone else's beliefs when they are different to ours (because ours are always legitimate, right?) would need to result from: a) differences in empirically derived facts; and/or b) differences in ethically derived values.

I could believe, descriptively, that the earth *is* flat, but it is indisputable that it is round(ish). I could believe, prescriptively, that the earth *ought to be* flat, but I am unaware of any good reasons for this belief. The empirical and ethical bases of the shape of the earth have been resolved. It is not flat, and there are no good reasons for different beliefs about it. So, it seems entirely acceptable for me to be beliefist towards flat earthers and perhaps even to discriminate against them in other ways on the grounds that they are clearly a bit silly. Well, even here things are not entirely straightforward. Do you know *for sure* that the earth is round? I don't. I trust the experts who have 'confirmed' it to be so, and the images I have been shown. So, the legitimacy of a belief will typically turn on whether its evidential or ethical source is legitimate.

In principle, the academy provides legitimacy to the empirical bases of beliefs. But our ethics shape how we understand evidence and limit our ability to look at any question 'objectively'. During the pandemic, for example, most academics who spoke publicly were in favour of strict social-distancing measures, in large part, I'm sure, because of their own fear of dying. They sought to interpret emerging evidence in ways that showed how lockdowns would be effective in significantly reducing deaths from Covid. There was something approaching blind faith in restrictions when there was never any compelling evidence to show that they did much good,[56] and no evidence at all they were overall beneficial when their collateral damage to education, social development, economic activity, etc., was considered. It is now becoming ever clearer – as a handful of us said all along – that the benefits of lockdown were tiny in comparison to the harms they caused.

My experiences during the pandemic have led me to largely give up on the idea of scientists ever being objective. All of us have myriad conscious and unconscious biases that with the best will in the world lead us to interpret flaky evidence as 'truth'. We are all, academics included, susceptible to 'capture' by interests and interest groups that lead us to take supposition as science. We should certainly be suspicious of any claims to objectivity from organisations that sit outside universities. The Global Disinformation Index in the UK, for example, is a not-for-profit institution that claims to promote 'neutrality, independence and transparency' in news reporting. In fact, it targets outlets whose output it deems to be 'harmful' or 'divisive', which is precisely how some of us were characterised when we spoke out against lockdowns.[57]

It's plainly difficult, to say the least, for us to separate the wheat of a legitimate belief from the chaff of a misguided or pathological one – even based on good evidence never mind sound logic. Consider the belief in God. So far as I am aware, there is no evidence of the existence of a deity. On that basis, I'm disinclined to believe in God. But as any academic will tell me, the absence of evidence is not evidence of absence. And there are plenty of smart scientists of faith. So, while I'm as sure as anyone could be that God does not exist, I cannot *know* for sure. I certainly would not discriminate against anyone who believed in a deity, and some of my best friends are religious. None of them seek to impose their religiosity on me and I don't seek to impose my atheism on them.

Does this mean that any belief goes? Well, yes but no. On the one hand, you can believe whatever you like but, on the other hand, you must be willing to stand by its consequences. Preferences rely on us making choices between options where one is rarely categorically better than another in every possible way. Rather, we are faced with trade-offs between myriad costs and benefits. So, it follows, I contend, that any belief worth its salt must be alert to the full flow of these costs and benefits following from its enactment. Signalling my support for, or disdain towards, a belief is empty and childish if it is not backed up by the depth of a grown-up assessment of its effects. We discussed earlier how quick and costless it can be to signal your beliefs, and this is 'cheap talk' if it is not accompanied with a willingness to engage with the complexity of the issue.[58]

Requiring that I am willing to maintain my support for a belief when the going gets tough – when all its costs are laid bare – means that I have some intellectual skin in the game. The term 'skin in the game' is typically used in contexts where people have some financial risk (skin) at stake in a business decision (the game). Another phrase in these situations would be 'money on the line'. Nassim Taleb's 2018 book is about skin in the game in a wider sense to include reputational effects, but it is unclear precisely what kinds of risks need to be taken for someone's beliefs and behaviours to be taken seriously.[59] I shall simply refer to beliefs that are backed up by a willingness to accept that they come with costs as well as benefits as a legitimate belief. The risk here is that the costs of its enactment may exceed its benefits.

Let me give an example as this is feeling a bit abstract. I

might believe that no one ought to be a billionaire (which I kind of do) but I must also accept that this will create downsides associated with reduced incentives and tax avoidance. If I stand up and defend (close to) 100 per cent marginal tax rates for billionaires, then I must be willing to accept all the downsides associated with this belief. If not, then I should either shut up or change my mind. Or consider the belief articulated by several politicians during Covid that 'every death is a tragedy'. This is an empty statement. We are all certain to die. My second intellectual hero (after Professor Alan Williams) is Danny Kahneman, who died in March 2024 at the age of ninety. I did not think of his death as being tragic in any way. Neither did he. And certainly not in comparison to the death of a nineteen-year-old, which most definitely is tragic. The tragedy of death is conditional on several factors, including the age of death.

It could be argued that engaging with the complexity of an issue must also include engaging with those who see a rabbit when you see a duck. This would mean that a legitimate belief can only be held by someone who is not beliefist. How do you feel about that proposition? It might make sense on a belief-by-belief basis. I can dismiss the views of a pro-lifer if they deny the consequences of their views or if they are unwilling to engage with someone else about them. But we're just as interested in the spillovers from beliefism, remember, and it would be inefficient and most likely unjust for me to dismiss a pro-lifer's beliefs about another issue – unless they were intransigent and unwilling properly to engage with the consequences of their beliefs here too. At the risk of labouring the point, well-functioning societies will have a distribution of beliefs. We should therefore be willing to engage with all those who are willing to themselves engage properly with their own beliefs.

Determining beliefs

What is it that causes some people to see a duck and others to see a rabbit? Well, four distinct yet interconnected pathways have been identified as governing the formation and evolution of beliefs: 1) nature;[60] 2) nurture;[61] 3) exposure;[62] 4) norms.[63] The nature pathway roots itself in our biological and genetic foundations, significantly shaping our inherent tendencies and predispositions. You might naturally lean towards or away from caution, conservatism, convention, etc., based on how you are 'wired'. Given the human instinct to shy away from, well, instinct, we have perhaps been too quick to downplay the separate role of genes. Several studies show how important who we are is. Robert Plomin's *Blueprint* makes a compelling case for genes playing a critical role in shaping our traits and behaviours, illustrating how deeply embedded genetic factors are in determining so much of how we view the world, and by extension whether we see the image as a duck or a rabbit.[64]

Every Boxing Day my kids and I go into Brighton city centre and give food, drink and money to homeless people. A few years ago, when Poppy was nine and Stan was eight, we bought a homeless woman a cup of tea. She asked if she could have sugar in it. As we walked back to the café to get some, my kids had an exchange about the morality of us getting it (don't worry, they didn't frame it that way). My daughter thought it was ungrateful of her not to just thank us for the tea and then go and get her own sugar. In contrast, my son thought it entirely legitimate for her to ask us to get it. They both made good arguments for their perspective. They did not end up agreeing about what was the right thing to do, but they also didn't fall out about it. Well, they didn't punch one another.

My two children saw our interaction with the homeless woman through very different eyes, despite their similar upbringing. I'm sure those of you with two or more kids would have witnessed some significant differences in the ways they see the world. Examples like this serve to remind us that our beliefs can be deeply entrenched in who we are at a fundamental level. This complexity in belief formation underscores the necessity to delve deeper into the 'nature' pathway, to understand the intricate ways in which our genetic blueprint moulds our beliefs and responses to the world around us – including, perhaps, our degree of beliefism. It also serves as an important reminder that we would not have evolved very well as a species if everyone thought the same.

The nurture pathway encompasses the influences that upbringing, education and societal values instil in us during our formative years. Family traditions and teachings deeply influence religious beliefs; cultural conditioning nurtures our beliefs about gender roles and societal norms, and so on. We are bound to have treated our two kids differently, not least because one had fifteen months as an only child while the other never had that 'luxury'; and because one is a girl, and the other is a boy. Research has examined how religious beliefs, political ideologies and attitudes towards social issues are often shaped by the family environment. Using a unique qualitative dataset with 471 parents in the 1980s and their adult offspring more than a decade later, one study showed significant transmission of beliefs from parent to child.[65] Unsurprisingly, perhaps, transmission was moderated by factors such as the strength of parent–child relationships, the consistency of political messages within the family, and the broader political climate during the child's formative years.

The respective roles of nature and nurture have been hotly contested for centuries. The simple and complicated answer, rooted in epigenetics, is that they interact with one another to shape our beliefs. For instance, maternal care in early life has been shown to influence the genes involved in stress responses, which in turn affects behavioural outcomes and stress resilience in adulthood.[66] These findings highlight how even genetically similar individuals can develop different stress responses and, by extension, varying beliefs about the world based on their early experiences. Another relevant area is the study of cognitive development, where researchers explore how genetic predispositions interact with educational and social environments to shape intellectual beliefs and cognitive biases. A stimulating home environment combined with quality educational opportunities can enhance cognitive development, leading to different beliefs and better decision-making skills.[67]

The third pathway is exposure. It highlights the significant role that personal experiences and the media play in shaping and modifying our beliefs over time. My two children get their news from different sources and different social media platforms: my daughter via TikTok and my son from the Sidemen on YouTube. We can see some more differences emerging between them that would not be explained by the interaction of nature and nurture alone. Research in political science has shown the powerful role of the political system and political parties and leaders in shaping beliefs.[68] While there is good evidence to show that political elites can significantly influence the belief systems of the population through propaganda, the degree to which beliefs can be completely changed in such a 'top-down' way has perhaps been overstated. For example, a study on X/Twitter conducted around the European Parliament elections in 2019 in Spain showed no evidence that exposure to polarised content increased polarisation.[69]

The fourth pathway is norms. We have already seen that we want to belong, and we take on the beliefs of those around us. Recent research shows how our perceptions of race and religion are shaped by our local environment.[70] New research looking at movers in the US shows that there is an 8 per cent change in political allegiance in the *first year* of the move if the move is from an area that is majority Republican to one that is majority Democrat or vice versa.[71] Movers could be more politically malleable than people who stay put but, still, these are large and rapid changes from one party to another. As Dan Gilbert reminded me when we last spoke, in many ways, our beliefs are the ties that bind us together. A recent follow-up study explores how the political behaviours of US citizens are influenced by their childhood environments.[72] The authors found significant 'exposure effects' indicating that a person's political alignment tends to conform to the predominant political orientation of the county where they spent their teen years, which are formative in so many ways (including music taste).[73]

These pathways illustrate that our beliefs are largely determined for us rather than by us. I'm sure I got a large part of my own tolerance from my mum (her genes and/or how she brought me up). Even the social media platforms 'chosen' by my own children have much more to do what's fashionable in their peer group than 'free will'. But most of us like to believe that some of what we do, think and feel is volitional. The important point here is that this serves to legitimise the judgements that we make about other people's beliefs. When someone 'chooses' to be different to us, they bring our beliefism on themselves much more than if they had no choice but to be different. Again, perceptions are everything. You might not choose very much of what you believe but I believe you do, and this is all that is needed for my beliefism. I can, of course, be beliefist even if I think you don't choose your beliefs – just like a racist doesn't care much for the fact that we do not choose the race we are born into – but discrimination is so much more easily justified in the presence of agency (assumed or otherwise).

Deciding beliefs

Insofar as we do choose some of what we believe, we might expect those beliefs to be decided upon with considerable recourse to evidence. But the cognitive burden associated with considering any stimulus in more than one way, coupled with our dislike for the ambivalence of the real world, means that we rarely weigh up all the evidence before forming a judgement. The human species has evolved to be thrifty, seeking to conserve energy wherever possible, including attentional energy. We create habits, and we dislike broken routines. We like to keep things simple, and to avoid any attention-seeking confusion, complexity and uncertainty. Consider the number of times you have been asked a difficult question and have instead answered a much easier one.

So, rather than assimilating evidence to decide whether and in what ways a stimulus will be a duck or a rabbit, we instead rely on simple rules of thumb to guide us. These often come in the form of stories, or narratives. In various ways, our lives are *lived* in stories, rather than in facts about times, places and itineraries. Simple narratives, about our own lives and about the lives of others, are more interesting and memorable than endless details. The best way to memorise the order of a pack of cards is to associate each card with a person or place and then to go on a personal 'journey' through the cards. The kinds of stories that are most relevant to beliefism are the social narratives about how we *ought* to judge any stimulus.[74] For example, the social narrative of status requires that I judge a banker to have a better job than a builder (while the data on happiness by occupation suggests that builders might have better jobs than bankers).[75] When we think about any issue, we reach for a narrative that makes sense of it and which shapes our beliefs about it.

If there are two sides to any argument, duck or rabbit, then there are two competing narratives for each issue. Our chosen narrative will be influenced by the prevailing social narratives, as well as by the degree to which it allows us to signal our virtue. It is most likely to be a narrative that we already know well, and it will be told by people or groups with which we identify. Our chosen story will *feel* as if it's compelling, coherent, straightforward and strong. For those of you familiar with the Brexit referendum in the UK, can you remember the slogans of the Leave and Remain campaigns? I would put a shedload of money (and I do like a flutter) on most of you remembering the slogan 'Take Back Control' used by the Brexiteers. It's one of the most memorable and effective political slogans ever. The Remain campaign led with 'Stronger in Europe'. I had to look that up because I had forgotten it.

Think about some of the stories you believe to be true. That human–made climate change is increasing the earth's temperature more than natural causes; or that income inequality is increasing? Do you know for sure yourself that these things are true? Almost certainly not unless you have specialist knowledge in these areas. You trust the people who tell you. You are more likely to trust sources of evidence and ethical arguments that you consider as having authority and expertise in the relevant domain. You may trust climate scientists for climate change data but not for evidence pertaining to the gender pay gap, and vice versa. Trust and expertise are the two big hitting elements of an effective *messenger*.[76] The extent to which you trust a source of information and how credible you consider it to be will also be determined by how much you *like* the messenger. The point for beliefism is that the simple messages conveyed by an effective messenger are likely to be much more duck- or rabbit-like than conveyed through different communication channels, or by the evidence itself.

Arguably, we have now reached the point where we don't decide whether we agree with an opinion until we hear who is saying it. Consider Marcus Rashford's successful campaign for free school meals for disadvantaged children in the school holidays in the UK. The recommendations were originally made by Henry Dimbleby, an old Etonian and CEO of the Leon food chain.[77] His plans were initially criticised by many on the left because, to put it bluntly but no less accurately, he's 'a posh bloke who doesn't know anything about the lives of poor kids'. The very same critics then strongly supported the very same recommendations when Marcus Rashford, the black footballer from a poor background, got involved. This provides further evidence of how our beliefs are decided upon in large part by the people with whom we identify and much less by the merits of the arguments relating to the issue at hand.

4

Daydream believer

It's about time I said a bit more about whether our beliefs affect our lives in ways beyond who we surround ourselves with. We vote, differently, of course, but does this affect our lives in arguably the most substantive way – through our happiness? It would be a lot easier to motivate reducing beliefism if less of it made people happier directly and not only through better decisions. As we shall see, the evidence is scarce and equivocal. Regardless, being less beliefist requires that we face up to the psychological hurdles and behavioural biases that drive us towards beliefism. Let's take each of happiness and behaviour in turn before we move on to the interventions in Part 2 that might be effective in reducing beliefism and its harmful spillovers.

Happily beliefist

Since happiness is partly determined by expectations, let me try and manage yours downwards a bit. There isn't very much

evidence on how beliefs directly affect happiness. Having
your beliefs 'win' matters, though. Evidence from the 2010
UK election shows that supporting the winner of the election causes a significant boost to happiness. But it only lasts
for a couple of months.[78] Similar research in the US found
that electoral losses have a negative effect on the happiness of
partisan losers immediately after the election, but the misery
lasts for about a week.[79] This reversion to baseline happiness
is consistent with tons of evidence showing relatively quick
adaptation to most stimuli. One study using panel data (i.e.,
data on the same people over time) from the last four US presidential elections showed the importance of expectations: the
effect of elections on happiness is much more negative, and
longer lasting, for those that expect to win and then lose.[80]

Looking at the effects of happiness on elections, research suggests that the electoral fate of governing parties is
significantly influenced by the national economy's performance – and by the national average for life satisfaction.[81]
Higher levels of life satisfaction are associated with increased
vote shares for incumbent parties. The study uses data from
the Eurobarometer series of opinion surveys and analyses
elections in fifteen EU countries since 1973. There is a clear
positive relationship between life satisfaction in the run-up
to elections and the electoral success of governing parties. A
further study attempted to explain Donald Trump's success
in the 2016 US presidential election.[82] Drawing on a large
dataset covering over 2 million individual surveys, aggre-
gated to the county level, the results show that low levels of
happiness are strongly predictive of Trump's victory, even
after accounting for an extensive list of demographic and
ideological variables.

If we're all happier from living in our 'belief bubbles', then
beliefism can be more easily justified. So, what evidence is

out there? Well, there is some evidence that hostility towards people who disagree with you politically can negatively affect your health, which may then affect your happiness. A study of nearly 5,000 Americans conducted in 2016 found that, while hostility might drive political engagement, which is typically associated with health benefits, the negative impact on health due to stress and negative emotions outweighs these benefits.[83] Another study from the US found that those participants who *perceived* that polarisation had increased were about 50 per cent more likely to develop anxiety and depression than those who perceived no change in polarisation.[84] These are important findings but should be treated with caution: changes in polarisation and mental health may both be caused by a third factor such as changes in optimism about the economy or personal characteristics. Optimism has itself been shown to be associated with happiness.[85]

There has been an increase in reports of negative emotion around the world since the financial crash in 2008.[86] The details and the size of the effect differ across countries but the general tendency to report more worry, stress, sadness and anger is pervasive. Several factors are likely to have caused this increase, including more instability in the world, greater fear of war or climate disaster, increased social media use, perhaps, as well as greater willingness to report negative feelings. I suspect that polarisation won't have impacted emotions too much, but that the increase in negative emotions has played a significant role in increasing affective polarisation. We are more likely to judge others harshly if we are not feeling so happy ourselves. We need more studies designed to test for causality in both directions.

There can be little doubt that the health of those on the receiving end of beliefism will suffer. The effects of racism will be much stronger, of course, but its harms illustrate how

being discriminated against can affect us. Discrimination-
related stress can lead to inflammatory reactions in the body,
leading to immediate health problems and chronic diseases
over time.[87] The health impacts of racism extend beyond
those who directly experience discrimination. Observing
racism can erode self-confidence and mental health in
children, affecting developmental milestones and academic
achievement.[88] This is especially true in cases where discrimination affects the children's parents, with studies showing
that parents who have experienced unfair treatment are more
likely to have children with behavioural issues.

Without much evidence on the relationship between
happiness and beliefism, we can look to the relationship between personality traits that we might expect to be related
to happiness and beliefism. The big five traits are openness,
conscientiousness, extraversion, agreeableness and neuroti-
cism (I remember them by the word ocean). The personality
trait that is most likely to be associated with less beliefism is
openness, which is defined in terms of people's willingness to
have new experiences, embrace change and be receptive to
new ideas. Openness is also the trait that, in general, is *least*
associated with happiness.[89] This is not to say it's unimportant
for happiness, it's just less important than the other traits, particularly extraversion. One study of Chinese college students
did find that openness to experience significantly predicted
happiness, but higher levels of openness were associated with
a greater propensity to experience awe, i.e., an overwhelming
feeling of admiration or wonder.[90] So, while openness might
make you less beliefist, it probably isn't going to do a great
deal on its own for your happiness.

The case for less beliefism based on happiness, then, is not
exactly overwhelming. Indeed, some people might be made
worse off in the short run from being less discriminatory

against people with different beliefs. But discrimination can still hurt those on the 'giving' end. Feeling hostile is rarely a nice feeling.[91] Less beliefism will result in less affective polarisation, which will be good for happiness. And those on the receiving end are likely to benefit by much more, so there will be less overall suffering in the world from less beliefism. We know that our own happiness is affected by the happiness of those around us.[92] Perhaps most importantly, a reduction in beliefism spillovers will mean that more efficient and innovative decisions will be made, which will increase happiness. So, even in the absence of good causal evidence, there is still a pretty decent prima facie case for reducing beliefism. There are some significant psychological barriers to increased tolerance, though, which we need to face up to before we can think about interventions to reduce beliefism.

Getting over ourselves

Reducing beliefism and its spillover requires that we accept some fundamentals of the human condition. The first, as noted above, is that we don't 'decide' on very much. You make thousands of decisions every day. Your brain makes this more manageable by automating most of what you do. It takes cues and clues on how to respond from your immediate environment. When I use the word environment here, I'm using it to mean the very 'local' cues and triggers that activate your unconscious, automatic and emotional brain (your 'system 1'). French music playing in a supermarket is an environment because it might nudge you, largely without your conscious awareness, towards buying French wine.[93]

While most of us would like to believe that we act volitionally with a clear logic, and with full activation of our conscious and deliberative 'system 2', we must accept the powerful effects of our instincts and emotions if we are to interact with those who are convinced that they see a rabbit when we strongly see the issue as a duck. Even when you think you've made an 'executive' decision it's often better described as system 2's 'execution' of what your system 1 has already decided for you in response to contextual influences. Think about how you will often post-hoc rationalise a decision. The contextual influences and cognitive justifications that we follow are rarely benign.

In much the same way as Daniel Kahneman has shown that most of the behavioural biases lend themselves to more hawk-like as opposed to dove-like actions in international negotiations, some of the core characteristics of the human condition will lead us to being beliefist.[94] There will be enormous differences between individuals in the degree to which we 'suffer' from each of the effects. There will be even greater differences, perhaps, between us in how much we perceive ourselves as being subject to them. But whatever the extent of your beliefism, or perception thereof, you will succumb to the effects simply by dint of being a human being. Reducing beliefism and its spillovers requires that we start by accepting that we are all 'wired' to like people who agree with us more than those who disagree, that we don't like ambiguity, and that we can get quite defensive when our views are challenged.

One of the main sources of adopting an entrenched position is the perception that to be seen as anything other than certain about an issue will be seen as a sign of weakness or, worse, ignorance. And yet admitting uncertainty or a lack of knowledge can enhance credibility and trustworthiness. Studies have shown that children learn better from someone who openly expresses uncertainty. For example, when children were taught about cause-and-effect relations with objects that worked only sometimes, they understood better from adults who communicated this uncertainty. Conversely, overconfidence, especially when proven wrong, can undermine trust. Children were less likely to trust an adult who confidently provided information that sometimes turned out to be wrong.[95]

People high in intellectual humility, who admit to not knowing, are more likely to consider a broader range of ideas. I know that fear played a large part in how most of the academy responded *en masse* to the threat of Covid, but I suspect that the confidence that some had in lockdowns was born out of a sense of insecurity. When I started writing about the collateral harms of social restrictions very early on in the pandemic, and always in a very respectful way, a senior academic at the LSE emailed to say that I should desist from this work as my comments would add to the death toll from Covid. In the face of such uncertainty, I admit to being a little jealous of his faith in lockdowns, but mostly troubled by his zealousness. So, I responded very politely saying that I would love to debate the issues with him in a forum of his choosing. He didn't reply.

This is also where our (mis)perceptions of others can come in. If I think your intransigence on a given issue signals your strong beliefs about it, then I might think that there is no point in engaging with you on it. As a rule, we are likely to think of others as being more dogmatic than us, not least because of the pervasiveness of the fundamental attribution error. We each see ourselves as tolerant and others as intransigent, and so no dialogue takes place – even though each of us might be willing to engage, at least to some extent, with one another. And yet it's almost impossible for *me* to contemplate reaching out to *you*. Moreover, we each imagine the psychological cost that would come from someone less worthy rejecting our initial move at dialogue. So, we each retreat further into our silos in much the same way as the two sides in international disputes often do.

Changes or trends in some aspects of our egos are likely to have led us to becoming increasingly beliefist over time. Consider the rise in perfectionism, which is defined as 'having excessively high personal standards and overly critical self-evaluations'. As my colleague at LSE, Tom Curran, has convincingly shown, the number of people who report being a perfectionist in these terms has increased significantly across the world over the past few decades.[96] Perfectionism might sometimes sound like a good thing, but it comes from a place of insecurity: from an inability to accept when something is good enough and an unwillingness to accept any criticism. A perfectionist is arguably more likely to be beliefist because it is much safer to stick to your own views or group rather than risk being exposed, internally or externally, as someone who doesn't have all the answers.

Have you heard of the dark triad? It refers to an unholy trinity of personality traits: Machiavellianism (highly manipulative), psychopathy (a lack of empathy) and narcissism (pathological self-regard). All of us are a bit of each, some of us score highly on one or two, and a small percentage have the dubious distinction of scoring highly on all three. Machiavellianism and narcissism have been linked to perceptions of one's qualifications for a political career and a desire to run for office. Psychopathy and narcissism have also been found directly to influence political participation. Interestingly, narcissism is associated with higher political interest but lower political knowledge. It appears that Machiavellianism is not associated with happiness, and psychopathy negatively so, while the narcissists among us are happier.[97]

Just like perfectionism, we have seen a rise in these traits over time, most notably narcissism. The endorsement rate for the statement 'I am an important person' has increased from about one in ten in the 1950s to around nine in ten nowadays.[98] Not every one of these respondents is a full-blown narcissist, of course, and it's healthy to think of oneself as a little bit special. But the average person is becoming ever more 'special' over time. Narcissists are vulnerable, even if on the outside they can sometimes appear self-assured. The more we seek to convince ourselves that we're right, that we're better than others and that we deserve to be admired, the more likely we are to be beliefist. What other people think is less important than what I think, so why bother listening to them?

To elevate themselves, some narcissists will feel the need to bring others down. The rise in narcissism may then go some way towards explaining the rise in negative feelings towards the out-group, which has been the biggest cause of the increase in affective polarisation. This is especially true for online interactions, where people can post abusive comments at almost no personal cost but significant gain to their own fragile sense of superiority. Despite their vulnerability, narcissists do not garner much sympathy. My wife, who you'll recall is a psychotherapist, likes working with narcissists because they often struggle making and keeping relationships. She says that she can help them with this, and this aligns with research indicating that therapeutic engagement with narcissists can help them improve their relational skills and reduce some of their more disruptive behaviours.[99]

Unlike my wife, most people often dismiss the views of a narcissist because they can rub people up the wrong way with their 'showing off'. A cycle of beliefism is then created: I don't like you, so I don't like your beliefs, which then feeds into you disliking me, which fuels my dislike for you, and so on. But listening to narcissists, despite their challenging traits, can have benefits. For example, narcissists' need for admiration and recognition can drive them to perform well in leadership roles, where their overconfidence might be perceived as competence by others. This can enhance their status and, in turn, lead to a more motivated and resilient approach to challenges. Listening to the beliefs of people we don't like can be hard but also rewarding if we can put our own egos to one side. I won't pretend that I find this anything other than fucking hard.

Our egos don't sit in isolation: they play out in our interactions with others and in the groups to which we belong. Dominant, and sometimes narcissistic, characters with big (but often quite fragile) egos will often seek to take charge in work and social settings. But there is no reason to suppose that a big ego is correlated with 'better' beliefs. This reminds us that it's hard for any individual to swim against the tide of beliefism, especially if the current is getting stronger over time. A willingness to listen to those who disagree with us might come largely from collective action and redesigning the landscape of our interactions but, in a world of fragile egos and dominant characters, and where perfectionism and narcissism are on the rise, it is even more important that we try, so much as we can, to show some humility about our own beliefs, and respect for what others think.

5

Moving on

That's *taking sides* dealt with. So, it might be worth taking a few moments to consider your key insights or takeaways from this first part of the book. Let me restate my central aim in this book: to contribute towards us each being less discriminatory against people with different beliefs to us. Reducing beliefism and its associated harmful spillovers is a laudable aim at any point in time, I think, but especially in a world where social media is changing the way we engage with one another and where moral dualism, anti-identity, virtue signalling and affective polarisation all appear to be increasing in ways that are impacting negatively on human decision making and on happiness.

Against this background, I hope that you might start thinking about beliefism a bit more – and use that word mostly alongside, but sometimes in contrast to, the other 'isms' that are used to define various forms of discrimination. Are you more beliefist than you thought? Or less so? Is it clearer why it's both important and difficult to be less

beliefist? Being less beliefist offers significant personal benefits such as increasing our ability to consider a broader range
of ideas, which can foster intellectual humility and improve
relationships by making us more tolerant and tolerable. There
are myriad social benefits from less beliefism too. Parents will
proudly say that their kids are very different to one another,
and we should want to say the same about society. Well-
functioning families and societies celebrate difference and
are all the better for it.

Unfortunately, less beliefism is far from a straightforward
challenge. We need to overcome the natural human tendency
to favour those who agree with us and the psychological need
for certainty and consistency, which can make it hard for us
to update our beliefs, including our views of other people and
groups, even when faced with compelling evidence to do so.
We are drawn towards forming, and being in, groups in all
walks of life where we can all nod along in agreement with
one another rather than shake our heads in disagreement.
Going with the grain of our human nature will frequently
lead us to sort into ducks and rabbits and to be hostile towards
those who see the other animal. Moreover, it's generally
easier to have someone or another group to blame for how
shit things are or for how you feel. There's a strong cognitive,
emotional and social tide of beliefism to swim against if we
are to become more tolerant.

So, the only effective way to reduce beliefism and its
harmful spillovers is to make it easier for us to be less beliefist
without having to think too hard about it. Even then, 'tolerance by design' isn't going to get us very far if we approach
every situation with a closed mind. Contexts can nudge you
around, but I don't think that they can fundamentally change
your desires. And even if they could, I don't think they should
be allowed to. There are ethical limits on how far nudges

should be allowed to go. So, at a minimum, becoming less beliefist requires that you at least have a weak preference for being so – a preference that will align to there being some individual and societal benefit from reducing beliefism. I know you do have this preference, so let's now EMBRACE the interventions that enable us to begin *breaking sides*.

Part 2

Breaking Sides

6

EMBRACE it, now

We have gone some way towards understanding the causes and consequences of beliefism and can now look towards interventions that have the potential to reduce beliefism. We cannot simply think ourselves less beliefist. We might think that we like a challenge, but we really don't: the path of least resistance is most often the preferred route. Willpower is weak but, thankfully, design power is strong. It is possible to make a habit of being less beliefist – to be tolerant by design. I will gather up the ways of designing environments to reduce beliefism under a new checklist: EMBRACE. The word itself means to accept something willingly or enthusiastically. So, it's an apposite mnemonic.

My intention here is to provide an evidence-based framework from which you can come up with innovative ways to reduce beliefism in your lives, families, clubs, workplaces and organisations. A checklist allows us to think clearly and carefully about what to do to reduce beliefism but, in so doing, it does not consider combinations of elements that may be more effective together than using one element in isolation. The best-shot interventions probably won't involve all elements as this could be overkill, cause confusion and potentially even increase beliefism rather than reduce it. But an intervention might combine two or three elements, so please keep this in mind as we go through each letter of EMBRACE in turn. Here are the elements of EMBRACE:

Environment	We need to emphasise situational factors.
Mistakes	We need to be allowed to make mistakes, and to learn from them.
Bonding	We need to remember that we are similar in so many ways.
Reason	We need better evidence and more coherent narratives.
Affect	We need to improve our emotional reactions to perspectives and people.
Collection	We need a diversity of people and perspectives in decision making.
Exposure	We need to spend more time with people who disagree with us.

Before getting into the elements, and at the risk of labouring the point, recall that we are aiming to reduce beliefism and its spillovers, and not to change beliefs to produce a consensus. We can think of EMBRACE as seeking to shift the whole distribution of beliefism 'leftwards' towards less beliefism. Irrespective of how tolerant and open-minded each of us might be, we are all prone to some degree of beliefism that is likely to be more than what is optimal for effective decision making as individuals, and in corporations and policymaking. You might consider EMBRACE as being analogous to a strong wind that pushes you in one direction but does not push you over. But unlike a strong wind, it will mostly push you in ways that you do not notice but nonetheless are thankful for.

7

Environment: we need to emphasise situational factors

Any attempts to reduce beliefism must necessarily draw on the proclivity of the human condition to go with the flow of the contextual factors that shape so much of what we do, think and feel. This means that education programmes, which seek to change the way we think in very deliberative ways have, at best, marginal effects on behaviour. Moreover, I challenge anyone to find an effective education or information programme that hasn't been most effective for those who start off better educated and informed in the first place. So even effective education programmes will serve to widen any education gap.[1] Consider university-level initiatives designed to foster a more tolerant campus environment by educating students about the importance of diversity and inclusion. It has been shown that students with a higher level of prior exposure to diversity are more likely to engage with and benefit from the content.[2] Where there are compelling grounds to change behaviour, I have generally found it much more effective to nudge them to act differently than to inform them to do so.[3]

The environment can be changed in subtle ways to reduce beliefism. In a series of experiments in the US, over 1,700 people took part in a study in which half (the treatment) were primed by images and statements consistent with being American, and half received no such prime (the control).[4] Both groups were then asked about their 'warmth' towards their own and the opposing political party on a 0–100 'thermometer' scale where higher numbers indicate warmer feelings. Those in the treatment group were about five degrees 'warmer' towards out-groups than in the control group. To place this in context: the difference in out-group warmth between strong and weak partisans was nine degrees.

In an interesting experiment conducted in Rwanda, researchers tested the impact of a radio soap opera featuring messages about reducing intergroup prejudice, violence and trauma in two fictional Rwandan communities.[5] Compared with a control group who listened to a health radio soap opera, listeners' perceptions of social norms and their behaviours changed with respect to open dissent, trust, empathy and cooperation. While not directly focused on beliefism (very few studies are), it seems reasonable to suppose that a reduction in prejudice will be associated with a reduction in beliefism. It is worth noting that the radio programme did little to change listeners' personal beliefs. This reminds us that we can reduce beliefism without having to change people's beliefs in the process.

The ways in which problems are framed in the environment will play a critical role in the effectiveness of perspective-taking.[6] For example, framing an issue in terms of common goals rather than competing interests can make us more willing to compromise by highlighting shared values and the benefits of cooperation. Further, perspective taking and framing can be enhanced through various interventions, such as mediated contact, where individuals are exposed to narratives or media that portray out-group members in a more nuanced and empathetic light.[7] Structured dialogue sessions that promote perspective taking and utilise constructive framing techniques have been shown to reduce polarised attitudes and increase willingness to engage in compromise.

Attempts to nudge less polarisation can sometimes backfire. In a recent study, 1,000 people were paid to follow a Twitter bot for one month that would automatically retweet messages representing a political ideology opposite to their own.[8] Contrary to expectations, liberals became slightly more liberal, and conservatives became significantly more conservative. This study did not look at beliefism, and increased polarisation is not in itself a problem, remember, but it does suggest that simply presenting people with opposing viewpoints will not be enough to break down barriers. Backfire effects will be more likely when selective exposure is present.[9] This refers to our tendency to favour content that aligns with our beliefs and to avoid or dismiss content that goes against our beliefs. In filtering information through the lens of our existing beliefs, we can become more polarised. Moreover, as we saw earlier, social media can create echo chambers that magnify selective exposure.

There are lessons from how we deal with the related concept of situational blindness that can help us address selective exposure. Situational blindness is one of the most pervasive effects of the environment on behaviour.[10] It is when we pay attention to one small aspect of a decision, which may be salient at the time, but which might not be what really matters in determining good or bad outcomes. Consider the pilot on a plane who is getting ready for take-off. She has checked all the instrumentation and everything looks in order, so she gets going. But there is no co-pilot next to her. She has forgotten about this obvious but overlooked factor that contributes significantly to the safety of the flight. Surely, a pilot wouldn't take off without a co-pilot ... ? Well, this used to happen from time to time and flight safety was severely compromised. None of us can pay attention to everything. I'm sure you can think of several times where you've missed something important.

Aviation is one of the most evidence based and forensic sectors. Whenever there is a crash or a major incident, lessons really are learned to reduce the risks of future incidents. So, what did the airline industry do about 'solo flights'? Well, they came up with *checklists*. These draw the pilots away from situational blindness and towards situational awareness, whereby all the factors that contribute towards flight safety are considered. The checklists are quite simple because situational blindness can lead us to overlook some important considerations. Checklists – just like EMBRACE developed here – allow us to step back from the issue to take a more complete look at it. An important item for pilots to check is the presence of a co-pilot. As a result, planes no longer take off with only the pilot in the cockpit and, thankfully, fewer major incidents occur.[11]

Checklists are also used widely in medicine to reduce errors made by surgeons when they miss crucial information in their environment.[12] As with aviation, the checklists contain some quite simple information but serve to ensure that there is a full picture of all the factors that affect safety. If you go into hospital for surgery, you can expect to confirm your name and date of birth so that they know they are operating on the right person. Each item on the checklist serves to create a comprehensive overview of the factors affecting patient safety. The success of checklists in reducing errors and enhancing outcomes in medicine underscores the significant impact that structured information can have on mitigating the narrowness of attention. Inspired by the power of checklists, I developed a checklist for behavioural interventions some years ago, called MINDSPACE (Messenger, Incentives, Norms, Defaults, Salience, Priming, Affect, Commitments, Ego), which draws attention to some of the obvious but overlooked 'facts' of human behaviour.[13]

No other sector is quite like aviation, not even medicine and certainly not behavioural science, but having to make a case for *why* an item should be on a checklist will at least ensure that evidence, or the lack of it, is discussed. The processes of policymaking during the pandemic were crying out for checklists. Each time a draconian measure to limit social contact was put in place there were long discussions of the likely effects on Covid transmission rates. The impact on loneliness, educational inequalities and so much more besides hardly got a look in. And I'm talking about even being recognised, never mind any attempt to estimate these consequences. An important point here, so far as the aims of this book are concerned, is that discussions about which items should go on a checklist are likely to involve more detachment and less hostility than arguments about what the policy decision should be. So, we can expect less beliefism by embedding the process of checklist development into policy.

In general, if the processes in the environment are legitimate, then we can expect to see less beliefism. In relation to political and public policy issues, this is the role of democratic institutions. In liberal democracies, most people appreciate that competing beliefs are put to the test at the ballot box. Political parties put forward a manifesto, which contains many policy objectives that come together into a loose, over-arching narrative and presents their stories to the electorate. Each voter then decides whether, on balance and overall, they see things more like a duck or a rabbit. The legislature serves to ensure that the overarching duck and rabbit narratives both play some part in the formulation of policy. Most people will agree on the process by which disputes between competing beliefs are settled. I have been struck by how gracious Rishi Sunak was in defeat after the 2024 UK general election.

8

Mistakes: we need to be allowed to make mistakes, and to learn from them

It is impossible to go through life without fucking up, personally and professionally. The issue is not whether we make mistakes but rather how we and others deal with them. It seems that the modern world of online interactions is finding it hard to accept that all of us get things wrong from time to time. When I gave a talk at the Hay Festival in May 2019, in relation to my book *Happy Ever After*, I spoke about how single, childfree women were the happiest and healthiest population subgroup. I also emphasised that we can't claim that this is causal evidence as, sadly for academic research but understandably from every ethical vantage point, we do not have any randomised controlled trials, which assign some people to marriage and others to remaining single. Notwithstanding this very important point, men appear to be the biggest winners from getting hitched, despite the pressure of the social narrative surrounding marriage being on women to settle down.

Unfortunately, I also drew on my own analysis in which I had misinterpreted the 'spouse present' code in the American Time Use Survey (ATUS) to mean the spouse was there for the interview rather than present in the household. I thought the data showed that women were happier when their other half was looking over their shoulder as they completed the survey, but it meant that they were happier when their husband lived with them (as compared to being in the armed forces, prison, etc.). It was a completely innocent error of interpretation on my part. As soon as I was made aware of the mistake, I notified the *Guardian* and their article, which prompted the media interest, was amended. I informed my editor at Penguin so that the book could be revised, and I publicly discussed it. I basically did everything you should do following a mistake: admit it and put it right as best as you can.

I regret the error, and I'm happy that it was spotted. It is one of the many advantages of analysing publicly available data. Some people have sought to discredit my whole book based on this one mistake, but there are no other errors in there. I say this because you can bet your life that the people who didn't like what I had to say about the powerful social narratives that constrain so many of us would have pored over it all. It should also be noted that my error accounts for about one half of 1 per cent of the text in *Happy Ever After* (about 400 words out of around 80,000). Crucially and thankfully, the error in no way affects the substance of any of my arguments about how happy and healthy single, childfree women are. As I have gone to great lengths to make clear since May 2019, there is plenty of evidence to support the claim that single, childfree women are often the happiest and healthiest subgroup.[14]

But those who 'knew' marriage was good for women – who

already 'knew' the image was one animal not the other – did not accept my apology, taking to Twitter and blog posts to abuse and defame me. One American professor continues to draw attention to my mistake at every opportunity, despite, so far as I can tell, having conducted no serious research on the causes and consequences of happiness. This experience has served to remind me that we are living through an age where serious academic discussion can be drowned out by emotional reactions to evidence that does not conform with what some people (even those who purport to be academics) have already established as 'fact'.

One of the things that attracted me to the academy was to be able to inform important social and policy issues with robust evidence. It was probably what drew me to happiness research. I am very concerned that anyone witnessing how some people have treated me after a small error in my book was drawn to public attention will think twice before putting their own heads above the parapet, especially if their arguments and evidence go against the grain. Peer review is central to our work, but peer abuse, I contend, is making the academy a very small, boring, insular and increasingly irrelevant place. What I experienced was stressful but comes nowhere near the abuse hurled at other academics who haven't even made a mistake but simply come to view the image as a duck when some very vocal opponents already 'know' it's a rabbit.

If we are to break down barriers that exist between people and perspectives, we must create environments where it is possible to make mistakes, to learn from them, and to move on. In some senses, we should be celebrating mistakes because, as we can all attest, we learn much more from when we mess up than when we get things right. In making mistakes, we need to pay more attention to the lessons that can be learned from them rather than to the 'if only' of wishing we'd never messed up. We certainly need more space (literal and metaphorical) for mistakes to be seen as valuable learning opportunities and not simply as failure. My mistake did not directly result in me now using 'childfree' rather than 'childless', but being forced to reflect on my error caused me to consider several aspects of the marriage/kids debate, including how we refer to different groups.

One potentially impactful intervention in facilitating mistakes is fostering a *growth mindset*. This is predicated on the belief that abilities and intelligence can be developed through dedication and hard work – and by learning from mistakes. The focus shifts from a static view of intelligence towards a dynamic view, which emphasises continuous learning and adaptation. In one study in education, where most growth mindset interventions have taken place, around 400 seventh grade students (twelve- to thirteen-year-olds) in the US participated in eight sessions in which they learned that the brain could grow stronger and smarter with effort and learning.[15] They were taught that mistakes were opportunities for learning. Students who received the growth mindset intervention showed a significant increase in their mathematics grades over the course of two years compared to a control group that did not receive the intervention. Importantly, students in the intervention group also reported a greater enjoyment of learning.

It is worth noting that the growth mindset approach has not gone unchallenged. One meta-analysis (which brings together data from several studies) concluded that 'the apparent effects of growth mindset interventions on academic achievement are likely attributable to inadequate study design, reporting flaws, and bias'.[16] Another meta-analysis in the same journal issue 'found positive effects on academic outcomes, mental health, and social functioning, especially when interventions are delivered to people expected to benefit the most'.[17] The last part of this quote appears to drive much of the differences in the conclusions. If all studies are lumped together, then the average effects of growth mindset interventions are close to zero, but if the studies are partitioned into those that work and those that do not, then there is some suggestion that growth mindset interventions can be effective for students who are struggling the most. This further illustrates that how we approach data can drive our conclusions – and how our beliefs may well determine how we approach data.

Learning from mistakes is an important process outside of education too. Companies can cultivate a growth mindset such that employees see mistakes as opportunities for growth rather than as threats to their competence or worth. Recent evidence supporting the beneficial effects of embracing mistakes can be found in various studies across organisational behaviour, leadership and innovation management fields. Leaders who encourage an open dialogue about failures and view them as opportunities for learning significantly contribute towards creating a culture of trust, openness and continuous improvement.[18] We have seen how effective checklists can be, so here's a checklist, of sorts, to help organisations embed error management into their workplace culture:

a. Embed leadership modelling – leaders should openly share their mistakes and the lessons learned, setting a tone that mistakes are an acceptable part of growth.
b. Implement 'retro session' reviews – structured debriefs after projects or significant decisions, focusing

on what went well and badly, and avoiding assigning blame.

c. Create innovation spaces – environments where employees are encouraged to experiment, with the understanding that not every initiative will succeed.

d. Establish clear communication channels – encourage employees to share feedback without fear of retribution, e.g., through feedback sessions and anonymous reporting.

e. Implement psychological safety – cultivate a no-blame environment where mistakes are seen as opportunities for learning, visibly supported and practised by leadership.

f. Create learning opportunities from mistakes – develop a systematic approach to errors when they occur, e.g., through 'post-mortem' meetings.

g. Integrate error management into training and development – include modules on error management, resilience and adaptability in training programmes.

h. Set up support systems – provide support for employees who are navigating the aftermath of a mistake, e.g., mentors and peer support groups.

It's impossible for every workplace to embed all these features but, thankfully, small changes can have big effects and so it's important to do whatever is possible within the resource-constrained world of your workplace.[19] Moreover, signalling that mistakes are not just tolerated but to some extent even celebrated as important lessons will serve to enhance productivity. We have seen how powerful signalling can be, so think about how it can be used as a force for good. For organisations to innovate effectively, especially in fast-paced industries, they must be willing to experiment and accept that failure is often a step towards success. Experimentation is inherently risky – there are no guarantees that a new idea or method will work as intended. Failures and setbacks are inevitable when pushing the boundaries of what is possible. An innovator must have the freedom to prototype, test, receive feedback and iterate based on what doesn't work as much as on what does.

This is all well and good, but how does it relate to belief-ism, you might ask? Good question. I hope the good answer is that in viewing mistakes as lessons learned, we view the people who make mistakes differently. We move from taking one mistake as a sign that they are the kind of person who *always* makes mistakes, which is the typical response inspired by the fundamental attribution error (FAE), and towards seeing them as someone who, like all of us, *sometimes* gets things wrong. This means that we will listen to their views. We might be even more inclined to listen to them if they admit their mistakes and seek to put them right. We all make mistakes, so it's not really the messing up that matters, but rather the cleaning up. Think about your best friend. I bet they've made plenty of mistakes. But you've forgiven them. There may be some things that you would find unforgivable but, by and large, we should afford everyone the opportu-nity to mess up and genuinely to apologise if we're going to reduce beliefism.

9

Bonding: we need to remember that we are similar in so many ways

It's a cliché, but nonetheless true: there is much more that unites us than that which divides us. Very few of us are motivated by confrontation. So, it will make us less beliefist if we can remind ourselves of the similarities between the goals and motivations of the in- and out-groups. In so doing, we will be better placed to recognise that someone is not all good or all bad based on one set of beliefs, even if we feel strongly and differently about that issue. Around one half of the comments to a piece Steve Baker and I wrote for *The Times Red Box* about vaccine passports in 2021 related to his views on Brexit. Not only is it time to move on from Brexit but also to recognise that no one is defined by their beliefs on one issue. An appreciation of our similarities will go a long way towards mitigating the harms caused by splitting and by the fundamental attribution error.

A 2023 paper systematically evaluated twenty-five different

interventions aimed at reducing political polarisation among a large sample of over 32,000 participants across the US.[20] The interventions tested varied in approach, including strategies that emphasised common ground and shared identities between opposing political parties, narratives that presented relatable individuals from the opposing side, and efforts aimed at correcting widespread misconceptions about the beliefs held by members of the opposing party. The findings revealed that a significant number of these interventions were effective in reducing levels of partisan animosity. Interventions that showcased relatable stories of individuals from the opposite party, and which highlighted a common cross-party identity, were the most effective. For example, a Positive Contact Video intervention depicted a series of interactions between pairs of people with quite different beliefs, who are nonetheless respectful of one another.

Researchers at Harvard have developed a new game, 'The Co-operation Game' to tackle political polarisation by encouraging players from different parts of the political spectrum to engage in cooperative tasks.[21] The game is a series of quizzes and interactive exercises in which participants are exposed to viewpoints different from their own in a structured manner that promotes understanding and empathy. This approach aims to reduce partisan hostility by highlighting shared values and mutual interests, demonstrating that collaboration across divides is both possible and beneficial. The emphasis is on understanding that people can have different perspectives, but they come at the questions and challenges with the same underlying motivation to improve individual and social welfare.

Recall from Part 1 that when partisans think about 'Democrats' or 'Republicans', they think of the other side as less honest and less intelligent. They will also imagine more extreme and more homogenous stereotypes of these groups, leading to heightened partisan animosity. The reality is that such extreme individuals are quite rare. In one study of 1,000 people, respondents believed that 32 per cent of Democrats are LGBT (versus the actual 6 per cent) and that 38 per cent of Republicans earn over $250,000 per year (versus the actual 2 per cent).[22] These misperceptions were shown to be consequential, as they influenced partisans' hostility about the opposing party. But when they learned the facts about the opposition, their animosity significantly decreased. This suggests that partisan hostility is largely directed at the perceived extremists rather than the typical members of the other party, and that reminding people of the 'typical' partisan can reduce hostility.

We could also look to find similarities that break down barriers and which make us more receptive to different voices. We might share the same music taste, for example, as someone who disagrees with us about abortion rights, and discussing that shared interest might help us bond in ways that make it easier for us to listen to their views on other issues, and perhaps even on abortion. There is evidence that we judge people much more favourably when they share the same name or birthday as us.[23] So, we should explore innovative ways in which we might use this evidence to design environments that increase our propensity to listen to others, e.g., by setting up debates between people who share characteristics, such as music tastes, names and birthdays, that are unrelated to their beliefs. You might like to think about how you could arrange this in your workplace.

There are some obvious but often overlooked universal determinants of happiness that can be used to reduce beliefism. Music, dance, sports and humour can all be leveraged to express and explore different narratives, while at the same time reminding us that the elements of what it means to live well are to some large extent universal. In Place of War (IPOW) is an organisation that creates and facilitates music projects, workshops and festivals in conflict zones and communities affected by violence and social upheaval.[24] Their initiatives bring people together from across the divide and provide a platform for voices that are frequently marginalised. The musical engagements offer a constructive outlet for emotion and energy, which might otherwise be channelled into conflict. They serve to cultivate a sense of identity and community cohesion, which is often compromised in conflict situations. If music can reduce beliefism in war zones, it can surely work in the meeting rooms of firms and institutions.

One of the ways we have come together pretty much since time immemorial is through dance. Dancing with other people has been shown to release oxytocin, a hormone that helps us to connect and bond with them.[25] I fucking love dancing. I'm very excited to have recently connected with the founders of Daybreaker, who organise dance events in the US for people before they go to work.[26] As I write, they are embarking on The Purple Tour, a series of forty-odd Daybreaker events, bringing red (Republican) and blue (Democrat) together to dance and to increase voter turnout at the US Presidential Election in November 2024. This shows how dance can be used to enhance democracy (and to tackle loneliness, which is the aim of the Belong Center, established by Radha Agrawal, co-founder of Daybreaker).[27] The oxytocin and the other hormones dance releases, such as dopamine, serotonin and endorphins, can increase our bonding in ways that will undoubtedly also reduce beliefism.

Sport also holds a powerful capacity to transcend or reduce beliefism. PeacePlayers International (PPI) uses basketball as a tool for reconciliation in divided communities. PPI's core belief is that children who play together can learn how to live together. PPI operates in various regions with a history of conflict, including the Middle East, South Africa, Northern Ireland and Cyprus. Its programmes are designed to bring together young people from opposing sides to engage in joint basketball training and games. These activities are not just about playing basketball: they are structured to encourage dialogue and friendship. This is achieved by creating mixed teams from opposing sides of conflicts and incorporating facilitated discussion sessions. PPI has been shown to improve attitudes towards members of the 'other' group.[28] Not everyone likes playing sport, of course, but everyone could at least be encouraged to watch to cheer on their 'team'. Sport is one area where we can all agree to disagree.

One tool stands out as a potential bridge across the belief divide: humour. In a 2019 paper, two studies were conducted to test the effect of humour on reducing affective polarisation in a conflict environment that is about as important and current as it can get: the Israel–Palestine conflict.[29] In Study 1, 113 Palestinian-Israelis read a message ostensibly from an Israeli representative conveying the Israeli narrative of the conflict. Participants were randomly assigned to one of three conditions: a control with no humorous content, one with general humorous asides added, and one with humorous asides specifically targeting the Israeli speaker or Israelis (self-deprecating humour). The results showed that compared to the control, participants in both humour conditions perceived the Israeli source as more credible and agreed more with the message. Those exposed to self-deprecating humour expressed a greater sense of commonality with Israelis and a greater willingness to compromise on core conflict issues.

Study 2 replicated this with 225 Jewish-Israeli participants reading a message from a Palestinian representative. It added a fourth condition where participants rated unrelated jokes to induce a positive mood separately from the message. While positive mood alone had no effect, general humour again increased perceived credibility and agreement with the message. Contrary to Study 1, it was general humour, and not self-deprecating jokes, that fostered greater perceived commonality and willingness to compromise among Jewish-Israelis. The authors suggest this reversal may relate to power asymmetries, where self-deprecating humour by the higher-power group reduces perceived distance for the lower-power one, but not vice versa. Overall, the findings demonstrate how subtle humour can reduce beliefism in seemingly intractable conflicts. Rather than belittling the seriousness of the conflict, humour can serve as a way through what feels like an intractable issue of beliefism.

In educational settings, humour has been shown to be a powerful tool for engaging students, enhancing learning, and also encouraging students from diverse backgrounds to connect with each other.[30] To reduce beliefism in a classroom setting, a lecturer could incorporate humour into discussions, particularly when addressing contentious topics. By using general humour or even self-deprecating jokes, the lecturer can create a more relaxed atmosphere, encouraging students to feel more comfortable sharing their views. This approach can help break down barriers between students with differing beliefs, making them more open to considering alternative perspectives and fostering a sense of commonality. I will now justify my crap jokes in lectures as an attempt to do this.

The lessons learned here extend to a meta-analysis in 2021 that showed that managers can use humour to reduce stress and enhance leadership, group cohesiveness, communication, creativity and organisational culture.[31] The authors suggest that self-enhancing and affiliative humour are especially effective. The former refers to the ability to maintain a humorous perspective on life's challenges and difficulties, and the latter involves sharing jokes, funny stories and witty banter. In healthcare, humour has been found to lighten the atmosphere of high-stress situations, improve patient outcomes, and foster better relationships between healthcare providers and patients. It can serve to bridge gaps between different social classes and cultural backgrounds.[32]

It is important to note that not all humour is created equal. Aggressive humour, which mocks or ridicules other people or groups, could exacerbate divisions rather than reduce them – and make people less happy too. A 2020 meta-analysis looked at eighty-five studies, with nearly 28,000 participants, involving the relationship between different styles of humour and various measures of wellbeing (including anxiety, distress, depression and optimism). The results suggest that while affiliative and self-enhancing humour enhances wellbeing, aggressive humour reduces wellbeing.[33] The key lies in leveraging humour's unique ability to diffuse tension, foster empathy and encourage dialogue, thus making it an effective tool for bridging the belief divide. There is nothing more bonding than having a good laugh with someone.

Ah, perhaps this is why academia is a pretty beliefist environment – many academics take themselves way too seriously to laugh in work. This is sort of a serious point. We need to design specific elements of bonding into environments that are fit for purpose. If academics are serious people, then humour could rub them up the wrong way (as I continue to learn to my cost). But we can still seek to introduce more play and levity in the classroom in ways that stimulate intellectual discourse and curiosity. There is certainly more that can be done in universities to encourage debate about issues, like sport, where disagreement is not only accepted but where we can bond over disagreeing. This could then make disagreeing about 'big' stuff easier. I might get my next class of students to debate the proposition that 'Coldplay are the most overrated band since the Beatles'. Well, that's more a statement of fact than a proposition but you get my point.

10

Reason: we need better evidence and more coherent narratives

If we are to reduce beliefism, we need to remind ourselves of the reasons sitting behind different beliefs. Before you rightly point out that reasons only go a small way towards explaining our beliefs, what matters most for the discussion here is that we *think* that our beliefs are based on good reasons, and not so much on whether that is substantively the case. While much of human activity is governed by factors outside of our awareness, we can all offer good reasons for why we act, think and feel in the ways we do. We are all experts in being able to justify ourselves in ways that give us the appearance of consistency and coherence. If academics want the evidence that they produce to change anything, it must be backed up by a compelling and convincing story. This is an obvious thing to say, and we have previously discussed the power of narratives. But like so much that is obvious, it is often overlooked.

There are several ways in which we can ensure that the reasons for seeing the duck and the rabbit both get an airing. In one study in the US, before writing essays on same-sex marriage, participants were asked to consider the moral values of the political group they were trying to persuade.[34] Conservatives were asked to consider arguments for same-sex marriage based on patriotism and respect for authority. Liberals were asked to consider arguments against same-sex marriage based on equality and fairness. This moral reframing had a significant effect on the degree to which other people agreed with the writing. When we are required to articulate the reasons for someone else's beliefs, especially in our own 'handwriting', it becomes much easier for us to appreciate those reasons. This highlights how we need to immerse ourselves somehow in someone else's reasons for their beliefs rather than passively receive information about why others believe the things they do.

In a related way, a critical component of reducing beliefism through reason is *feedback* that is framed in ways that resonate with people's lives and their values. We should seek to embed both formal and informal feedback into decision making. In policymaking, for example, there should be standing bodies to oversee important decisions. There have been various calls for 'red team' challenges in learning the lessons from the pandemic. This is where a group is explicitly charged with challenging policy proposals. The Covid Inquiry in the UK is taking place as I work on this book. It has focused a lot on accountability, and the soap opera surrounding who hated whom and expletives in WhatsApp messages. *The* main lesson, surely, is for different beliefs and values to be fed into decision-making processes.

A potentially important mechanism through which feedback can impact upon beliefism is more open and inclusive science. For most individuals, high-level scientific knowledge is hard to grasp and inaccessible. This creates a 'defensive wall' between people and new scientific evidence. Over the past years, efforts have been made to bridge this gap, e.g., with Open Popular Science talks to communicate science to the public, and through citizen science projects which recruit volunteers to collect data to address real-world questions such as the effects of light pollution on the sky at night. These activities are not designed specifically to reduce beliefism but, in building important feedback mechanisms between citizens, scientists and policymakers, they reduce the 'distance', and by implication the hostility, between the various stakeholders in science. A note of caution here, though: recall our study discussed earlier showing that we can sometimes get carried away with our faith in scientists.

A related approach to inform, and be informed by, public opinion is *deliberative polling*, which provides participants with balanced information and the opportunity to engage in thoughtful deliberation. The process involves gathering a representative sample of the population, providing them with information on a specific issue, and creating a space for discussions and interactions with experts. Before they begin, participants complete a survey of their beliefs relevant to the group discussion. Participants then engage in facilitated small-group discussions, where they can share their views, ask questions and challenge each other's opinions. They can also pose questions to experts. After the deliberation, participants complete the same survey to measure any changes in their opinions, beliefs and attitudes.

Deliberative polling directly addresses beliefism by challenging participants to reconsider their pre-existing beliefs considering new information and the viewpoints of others. It ensures that feedback is formally embedded into the decision-making process. It serves to flush out the different ways in which evidence, narratives and feedback can all shape not only our own beliefs but how others can legitimately see a duck when we see a rabbit. I have some experience of working with Citizen's Juries, as they were called when I was working with the National Institute for Health and Care Excellence (NICE) on priority setting in healthcare in the 1990s. So, the approach has been around, in various forms and names, for quite a while. I was struck by the quality of the discussions and the ability of people to engage with different perspectives.

But – and it's a big but – we don't know whether 'hot' post-deliberation preferences revert to the 'cold' pre-process ones with which people came to the deliberation. It's striking how so few studies have sought to follow up a few weeks let alone months after deliberation. Indeed, it's striking that so few studies using any of the elements of EMBRACE have followed up with people at all. There are all sorts of reasons for this but most centre around the incentives of all involved to look only at short-term effects. There is little incentive in academia to go beyond the confines of an experiment and every incentive to write up the results for publication as quickly as possible. Similarly, policymakers are often only in their roles for a year or two, so they need to show 'quick wins' before they move on. Embedding long-term lessons and feedback into research and policy requires incentivising looking at longer-term effects.

We need more and better feedback in our personal lives too. This is challenging, of course, since most of the time we get positive feedback from agreement. Most of us would much rather stay away from the discomfort of disagreement. But we should try to find out how exposing ourselves to getting feedback about different perspectives makes us feel.

There is now tons of evidence to show that we are not very good at predicting how various stimuli will make us feel into the longer term. In general, we do not account for the fact that we adapt quite quickly to most stimuli and situations. We also tend to focus on the negative aspects of a change and downplay the upsides. In a study where people were asked to talk to strangers, they hated the idea but, much to their surprise, quite enjoyed the experience.[35] I'm assuming that the strangers quite liked it too. Similarly, we might fear different perspectives, but we might find out there are surprising benefits from exposing ourselves to them.

11

Affect: we need to improve our emotional reactions to perspectives and people

We can be reasonable creatures, but mostly we are reactive ones. We respond emotionally to many cues and triggers in the environment, including the beliefs of other people. The increase in affective polarisation that has been seen over the past few decades, and the hostility towards out-groups online, are emotional phenomena. So, affect — psychology speak for feelings — is an obvious element of a checklist designed to reduce beliefism. Notice the description above does not say that we need to *remove* our emotional reactions to perspectives and people but rather to *improve* those reactions. While being 'too emotional' is an insult, and much of standard economic theory is cleansed of feelings, it is also true that being 'devoid of emotion' can get us into trouble.

Several cool studies show that we can make some quite crazy decisions — such as continuing to pick from decks of cards that mean we will end up losing more money than we will win – when we do not get feedback for how those decisions make us feel.[36] These studies have led to the development of the *somatic marker hypothesis*, which posits that emotions guide all behaviour, including decisions that economists might classify as rational as well as the more obviously impulsive ones we might make when feeling aroused. Following from work with brain-injury patients, who have been rendered unable to feel the feedback from the consequences of their actions, somatic markers are thought to be processed in the ventromedial prefrontal cortex and the amygdala regions in the brain.[37] As ever, nothing in life is wholly good or bad.

The objective, then, is to *improve* our emotional reactions, so that they are fit for purpose. Fear is a particularly potent emotion in belief formation and beliefism. When we are afraid, we rely heavily on stereotypes and exhibit a decreased willingness to engage with conflicting viewpoints. In one study, participants were presented with scenarios or images that elicited feelings of fear (such as blood, injections, spiders, bugs and angry faces) towards members of an out-group, and their empathetic responses were measured through self-reports and neural activity patterns.[38] The study found that participants exposed to fear-inducing stimuli showed a marked reduction in empathetic engagement with the out-group members. Additionally, these participants were more likely to endorse negative stereotypes and exhibit stronger in-group biases, highlighting how fear can entrench existing beliefs and inhibit openness to alternative perspectives. Put simply, more fear, less empathy.

Positive emotions have been shown to play a significant role in so many aspects of life. This includes research demonstrating how high-arousal emotions significantly influence sharing behaviours online.[39] It turns out that awe and surprise can lead to posts going viral, and these feelings appear to be much more powerful drivers of virality than negative emotions. There is some suggestion that positive emotions broaden an individual's thought–action repertoire, which in turn helps to build their social and psychological resources. This is not without criticism, though, as recent research suggests that negative emotions can also increase the breadth of attention. It is likely that the differences are explained by motivation: some positive and some negative emotions can lead to us wanting to *approach* something, while others may result in us wanting to *avoid* it.

The point here is that, in the context of beliefism, happiness and related positive emotions have the potential to encourage more open-minded consideration of alternative viewpoints and foster greater empathy towards others. In his 2024 book *Supercommunicators*, Charles Duhigg emphasises the importance of using emotion in conversations to connect with others and reduce polarisation.[40] Emotional states play a critical role in the context of negotiations, from which we can make extrapolations to beliefism. Context always matters. Displaying anger, for instance, can signal strong commitment to a position and may lead to concessions from the opposite party, whereas showing happiness might foster cooperation and trust.[41] These emotional expressions, both deliberate and spontaneous, communicate vital information about intentions and expectations to the other party.

It would be surprising if most emotions had not evolved and been culturally selected for their adaptiveness in contributing to both individual fitness and group functioning. And perhaps because of the predominance of homophily in intellectual discourse, there is very little causal evidence on which emotions to activate for targeting beliefism. Notwithstanding the role for positive reactions, a case could surely be made for us all calming down a bit. The importance of calmness transcends mere emotional self-regulation; it becomes a foundational pillar for a society in which diverse perspectives can coexist and interact constructively. By understanding and harnessing the power of calmness, we can create and curate interactions where differences are not just tolerated but are engaged with in a manner that enriches our collective discourse and fosters a deeper sense of community and mutual understanding.

So, many of the interventions designed to reduce beliefism will require us to take the emotional equivalent of a deep breath. One way that people could stop themselves wading into issues online is to set a delay on their posts and ask for confirmation that they want to send it. A proverbial and a literal deep breath both enables us to detach ourselves ever so slightly from the immediate and emotional 'system 1' environment and engage conscious and deliberative 'system 2' processes. It takes around fifteen minutes for system 2 to engage properly again after system 1 emotions have been in charge.[42] All four of us in our household are very emotionally reactive and we have learned to walk away from a heated situation at home (well, OK, not all the time, but enough times to mean that we have stopped short of killing one another). We're also pretty good at making each other laugh to defuse a situation. We're all different, of course, and some people will not react so well to emotional reactions and will take longer to calm down once aroused.

Whatever the individual differences, there is some pretty good evidence that taking a break can reduce beliefism. One study involved psychologists and conflict resolution experts, and examined the role of time breaks in discussions, especially in contentious settings.[43] Participants from various political and social backgrounds engaged in structured debates with intentional time breaks. The study detailed two experiments to explore the impact of breaks during negotiation, focusing on reflective versus distracting breaks. Reflective breaks involved participants thinking about the negotiation process, their strategies and their opponent's perspective. In contrast, distracting breaks had participants engage in an unrelated task, such as assessing the layout of the local post office, to divert their attention from the negotiation. The results showed that reflective breaks often led to more entrenched positions whereas the distracting breaks led to more productive negotiations upon resumption. So, not all breaks are created equal. A 'proper' break is likely to be more effective.

I was quite dismissive of education programmes earlier, but they could be used to remind us of the 'hot–cold empathy gap', which refers to how we underestimate the visceral influences on our behaviour.[44] Think about how a job interview generally goes less well than you imagine: your answers in the heat of the moment are never quite as good as you imagine them being when you're in a cold state before and after. Education programmes that address this gap can equip individuals with strategies to better anticipate and understand the dynamics of hot states, improving interpersonal understanding and reducing conflicts. This could include discussions that encourage reflection on past decisions made in emotionally charged environments. This can be particularly effective in diverse environments where misunderstandings and conflicts may arise not only from differing perspectives but also in how different people emotionally react to those differences.

It's hard for us to remember when and how to take a break, though, especially in the heat of debate. So, this could be one item on a checklist in the workplace, or a Post-it note on your computer screen. Indeed, the art of pausing not only gives our brains a moment to reset but also serves as a bridge to better understanding. When emotions run high, they cloud our ability to see things from other perspectives. By stepping away, we create a psychological space that allows for emotional cooling and cognitive reappraisal.[45] This isn't just about stopping an argument; it's about enriching it. It's about returning to the discussion with a refreshed mind and perhaps a new viewpoint that wasn't apparent in the throes of disagreement. Moments of pause can become rituals of reflection, where 'thinking time' is as important as 'doing time'.

Mindfulness has been shown to impact upon the emotional conditions required for less beliefism. A meta-analysis of thirty-one psychology papers shows that mindfulness training reliably promotes compassionate helping, reliably reduces prejudice, and has positive effects in pro-social behaviours.[46] Controlled breathing has also been shown to impact upon precursors for beliefism.[47] One study involving forty participants showed that controlled breathing had significant effects on stress and cognitive clarity in tasks that required focused attention and emotional regulation. There was no direct test of beliefism in this study and note the small sample size, so we should be cautious about making any generalisations from it. I'm not a big fan of 'formal' mindfulness, and the thought of controlled breathing is enough to make me hyperventilate. Here, as elsewhere, we must be alert to individual differences when designing interventions. They could backfire if they rub some people (me) up the wrong way. But they are promising avenues for intervention nonetheless.

Conversational receptiveness (CR), backed up by 'good' feelings, offers one way of combatting beliefism. As the term implies, CR captures the extent to which individuals demonstrate openness to engaging with opposing views during conversations. To help improve emotional receptiveness in conversations, the HEAR mnemonic has drawn out the four

ways of expressing CR.[48] First, *hedge* statements. These are
phrases that soften assertions, showing that you're open to
other possibilities. Examples include 'I think . . . ' or 'It could
be that . . . ' Second, *emphasise* agreement. This involves highlighting areas of agreement before discussing disagreements.
It sets a positive tone and shows you're looking for common
ground. Third, *acknowledge* other perspectives. This is about
showing you understand and respect different viewpoints,
even if you don't agree with them. Fourth, and this is perhaps where positive emotions play the most significant role,
reframe to the positive. These strategies collectively soften the
emotional edges of conversation.

Managing emotions in the digital realm, including text-
based communications like emails, is vital for reducing
beliefism. Alongside taking a break, it's helpful to clarify your
intentions in your messages and to ask for clarification when
interpreting others' messages. The lack of non-verbal cues in
text-based communication can lead to misunderstandings.
Setting boundaries and knowing when to step away from
a conversation can be crucial – knowing when to hold 'em
and when to fold 'em, in the words of the Kenny Rogers
song 'The Gambler'. It never ceases to amaze me how long
people will spend emailing or messaging someone back and
forth, and how long their messages are when they do. Often
the situation will escalate completely unnecessarily. There
comes a time when it's time to end the conversation – either
completely or by simply picking up the phone and having a
proper chat to clear the air.

I've had my fair share of abusive messages about issues
ranging from my complete lack of interest in novels to the
white glasses I wear for speaking events. I don't engage with
the abuse because it would only fan the flames. But if I did
reply, it would be to ask the person abusing me what they

think underpins their reasons for abusing me. I'm nowhere near narcissistic enough or way too narcissistic – or maybe both at the same time – to think that the message has much do with me at all. Rather, it taps into something in their own lives or experiences that has been activated by something I've said or how I've said it, or how I dress, or whatever. Most of how people react towards us says more about them than us, and reminding ourselves of this from time to time can prevent us from wading into an argument in an aroused state or, more accurately, 'wrongly' aroused.

12

Collection: we need a diversity of people and perspectives in decision making

Well-functioning societies embrace difference. Effective decision making requires a collection of perspectives. Well, context matters. Diversity is less important when the outcomes of the task are clearly specified. A 4 x 100 m relay team simply needs the fastest runners who can hand over a baton, and they can all think alike. But for most complex decision environments, like how best to increase productivity in the workplace, a diverse range of perspectives is essential. A compelling example of how diversity in perspectives improves performance in complex decision-making environments can be found in the financial sector, particularly within investment fund management. There is some evidence that investment funds managed by diverse teams, incorporating various backgrounds, often outperform those managed by more homogeneous teams.[49] For reasons of efficiency and fairness, there has been emphasis placed on diversity of characteristics over the past few decades, such as ensuring that different genders and races are represented.

This is not a book about diversity in the workplace and different data show different effects (and, as ever, much depends on the beliefs that academics bring to bear) but I think it's fair to say that diversity of characteristics, on balance, has a quite small but nonetheless significant effect on the bottom line. A recent meta-analysis of 106 articles published between 1997 and 2021 synthesised the impact of cultural diversity within top management teams (TMTs).[50] The study highlights how cultural diversity in TMTs significantly affects various organisational outcomes through complex mechanisms that involve both enabling and inhibiting factors at individual, team and organisational levels. Diverse management teams are also better equipped to understand and cater to a global customer base, enhancing customer satisfaction and loyalty. Leaders who exhibit diversity and inclusivity in their management practices can appeal to a wider array of customers and clients, benefiting from a deeper understanding of diverse markets and consumer needs. Leaders who embrace and manage diversity effectively foster an inclusive environment where all employees feel valued and empowered to contribute their unique perspectives.

Alongside gender and race, and disability and sexual orientation, we must seek to hire more openly working-class people into senior positions, and not just those of working-class origin. It is well documented that working-class *perspectives* are grossly underrepresented in high-status occupations. This is distinct from the underrepresentation of working-class *people*. It is important that people from all walks of life have opportunities to achieve success in their chosen careers. But this must be coupled with them being allowed to retain beliefs and behaviours that they may have grown up with but which they might be expected to leave behind when they become successful. Or indeed *forced* to leave behind if they want to be successful in their chosen career. Working-class people still have to choose between either fitting in or fucking off. The absence of class from the list of protected characteristics does not help in this regard.

But what matters most of all for this book is whether and in what ways a collection – and acceptance – of different beliefs leads to better decisions. Sometimes beliefs correlate with characteristics, and so diversity of the latter results in the former, and in more effective decisions. It has been shown that gender mixed groups generally perform better than all-male or all-female groups. In an experiment with over 200 undergraduate business students in the US, racially diverse groups outperformed homogeneous groups in a murder mystery exercise that required sharing information to succeed.[51] This study underlines how diversity fosters a broader range of perspectives and creative problem solving. It should be noted, of course, that what applies in an American university might not be generalisable elsewhere.

What we believe may sometimes be uncorrelated with who we are in terms of gender, race, age, social class, sexual orientation, etc. So having more women, ethnic minorities and so on involved in decision making may not in itself promote a diversity of perspective. Indeed, we may become complacent in thinking that we've 'nailed it' by having different backgrounds represented. We have already seen what a powerful and pervasive beast groupthink can be. So, groups in environments that do not actively encourage the expression of diverse viewpoints – that are not inclusive as well as diverse – will typically converge around shared beliefs or norms, irrespective of the degree of demographic diversity in the group.[52]

In academia there is increasing recognition, and mounting criticism, that the majority of faculty at the leading institutions are liberals with progressive agendas. I would say that for the first half of my time as an academic (until around 2008), most of my discussions with colleagues were of the research or policy question at hand. There might have been some reference or other to the politics involved but nothing much and certainly not in a way that presumed too much about the political affiliations of those involved in the discussion. Since then, it has become quite commonplace for academics to mock right-leaning perspectives. This is not so surprising. When I was a fresh- (well, acne-) faced junior academic in 1991, about two-thirds of academics said they voted Labour. In a 2017 survey by the University and College Union (UCU) in the UK, only about 6 per cent of respondents self-identify as centrist-right to right.[53]

This might be great news for the academics who can speak out and pat themselves on the back for what they might label as their progressive views, safe in the knowledge that few people will challenge them. It also allows academics to become more directly associated with advocacy for so-called progressive causes, and directly to impact public discourse and public policy. But it's really bad news for the quality of academic debate, for the selection of research questions, and for the impact of research on wider society. We need radically to shift the norm in the academy so that it is more representative of wider society. And if we can't do that, then we need to ensure that those with minority views are listened to and not mocked.

One possible solution to a lack of diversity of thought in academic research is through what Danny Kahneman has referred to as 'adversarial collaboration'.[54] This is where academics with openly different beliefs about an issue work together to produce evidence that will go some way towards settling the dispute about the facts relating to that issue. I am seeking to embed adversarial collaboration into my own work. But it does require people to change their minds based on better evidence and we know how hard this is for all of us. It also requires that diverse beliefs are present in the first place, which brings us back to ensuring that the academy has the requisite degree of diversity of thought. When I created the Department of Psychological and Behavioural Science at the LSE, I made several faculty appointments and I would have loved to have been able to hire according to the diversity of belief. At the same time as having lots of voices in my ear about diversity of characteristics, I heard literally nothing in relation to diversity of beliefs.

Inside and outside of the ivory towers, an evidence-based intervention for enhanced diversity in a workplace once the hiring process is complete is *cognitive diversity*. This refers to the differences in knowledge, perspectives and problem-solving strategies among individuals in a group. It goes beyond demographic diversity to focus on the diversity of thought processes and approaches to addressing challenges. A 2015 meta-analysis revealed that cognitive diversity interventions can significantly influence team dynamics.[55] Cognitive diversity has a more direct impact on a group's effectiveness than demographic diversity alone. It involves five main steps:

1. Selection of participants – participants are selected based on their diverse cognitive styles, which can be assessed using various psychological tests and inventories.
2. Formation of groups – participants are assigned to groups ensuring a mix of different cognitive styles.

For example, some individuals might be more analytical, while others are more intuitive.

3. Problem-solving task – the groups are given complex, ambiguous problems to solve, which require
   considering multiple perspectives and potential
   solutions.
4. Measurement of performance – the performance of
   the groups is measured based on the quality of their
   solutions, the time taken to reach a decision, and the
   level of innovation in their approaches.
5. Assessment of group dynamics – observations and
   surveys are used to assess the dynamics within the
   groups, including how different perspectives were
   integrated, and any challenges faced in the decision-
   making process.

Cognitive diversity is by no means a silver bullet. Team
members who think differently can struggle to find cohesive
social bonds, as individuals may find it harder to relate to each
other's viewpoints and problem-solving approaches. This can
make it harder for members to feel a sense of belonging and
unity. It sounds obvious but cognitive diversity interventions
will be more effective when the team members really want
the process to work. As with many phenomena, there is likely
to be a sweet spot – or Goldilocks effect – when the amount
of diversity is just about right. Too little and it won't make
much difference; too much and it can backfire with too much
distance between team members. The returns on diversity
are likely to diminish for each incremental 'unit' of diversity
until further diversity becomes ineffective.

Diversity of thought can also be actively encouraged
through the decision-making process. This is referred to as
exposed cognitive diversity. The focus here is on manipulating

team members' understanding of tasks or systems, leading to diverse cognitive approaches within the team. In high-complexity tasks, teams with a mix of both procedural and knowledge-based understanding have been shown to outperform teams with a homogeneous understanding. In a study within Chinese academic research teams, researchers tried to measure cognitive diversity and its effects on performance.[56] The researchers began by interviewing academic team members to generate relevant scale items, eventually refining these into a fifteen-item scale, which was validated through exploratory and confirmatory factor analyses across several samples, confirming its structure and reliability. The study found that cognitive diversity as measured by the new scale positively correlated with increased team creativity and performance.

Beliefism, not diversity, is the focus of this book but studies of this kind highlight how the latter, by extension, serves to break down the former. In discussing workplaces, we must consider recent developments in the use of technology and, relatedly, modern practices in working from home. Technology can help and hinder work practices. Some of the key lessons from in-person interactions transfer across to online interactions. Clear communication, virtual team-building activities,[57] expert facilitation[58] so that diverse teams can contribute equally and effectively, and the appropriate use of anonymity options can all foster collaboration behaviours to enhance wellbeing, increase productivity and reduce beliefism. We're still navigating our way around virtual meetings, but they can feel, quite literally, very remote, which makes it doubly important that the main features of creating inclusive environments are designed into those meetings.

13

Exposure: we need to spend more time with people who disagree with us

One of the most widely cited ways to reduce beliefism is *exposure* to the out-group and their beliefs. Creating environments that promote positive intergroup contact has been shown to reduce prejudice and improve intergroup relations. Gordon Allport's contact hypothesis from the 1950s suggests that direct contact between members of different groups can lead to reduced prejudice and improved relations.[59] The context of the mid-twentieth century, marked by racial segregation, social unrest and the beginnings of the civil rights movement in the US, provided a fertile ground for Allport's theory. He was concerned with understanding the roots of prejudice and discrimination and was particularly focused on racial and ethnic tensions. His theory emerged from a critical analysis of the social dynamics that lead to prejudice, as well as a thorough review of existing psychological research and theories related to intergroup conflict, stereotypes and social identity.

Allport's theory has since been subjected to extensive empirical testing, with a significant body of research supporting its core propositions. Integrated schools and sports teams are prime examples of the contact hypothesis in action.[60] A meta-analytic review of intergroup contact, which included data from a variety of settings including schools, found that intergroup contact typically reduces intergroup prejudice.[61] In sports, the mere act of working together towards a common victory can break down barriers between individuals from different racial or ethnic backgrounds. An example of this is the integration of Major League Baseball (which had a 'colour bar' excluding black players until 1947) that not only challenged societal norms but also fostered camaraderie and mutual respect among players of different races.[62]

For the contact intervention to be successful, four conditions must be satisfied:

1. The groups should have goals that in some substantive ways are perceived by both sides as being shared.
2. The setting should also allow for the potential development of cross-group friendships, which is an important element in reducing beliefism.
3. The groups must perceive each other as having equal status to challenge existing stereotypes and promote respect.
4. There should be broad institutional support that would legitimise the interaction and reduce the risk of conflict.

Notice how conditions 1 and 2 are closely related to the principle of bonding; 3 reminds us that power dynamics are important; and 4 that the surrounding environment within which exposure takes place plays a significant role in any attempts to reduce beliefism.

The research on intergroup contact theory and its application provides several key findings. First, relatively short-term interactions can sometimes be effective. Experiments within community and organisational settings indicate that community service projects lasting several weeks or cultural exchange programmes over a few months can lead to improved attitudes towards out-group members and reduced prejudice. A meta-analysis found that interventions involving direct face-to-face contact, cooperative learning and extended contact (e.g., exposure to positive stories or media about out-groups) were effective in improving attitudes towards different ethnic groups both immediately and up to a year after the intervention.[63]

Second, and perhaps less surprisingly, longer-term exposure can be effective too. A recent study painted a nice picture of how reduced prejudice relates to reducing beliefism.[64] Using a combination of historical and contemporary data, the study focused on the impact of long-term exposure to foreign ancestries on natives' attitudes and behaviours. It demonstrates that sustained exposure to a specific foreign group, Arab Muslims in this case, can lead to decreased explicit and implicit prejudice against this group. The study also found a decline in support for policies and political candidates that are hostile towards Arab Muslims among individuals with prolonged exposure to this group. This change in political stance could also be interpreted as indicative of a shift away from beliefism.

Third, several studies reinforce the third condition of contact theory above: that for intergroup contact to work in reducing beliefism, the contact must happen across groups of

similar status.[65] In situations where the status hierarchy is pre-
served, the high-status group may not have as much incentive
to change their attitudes, and the low-status group may feel
their identity is threatened, potentially leading to increased
intergroup tension. In the very least, the interactions should
not reinforce existing hierarchies. This can be facilitated by
creating an environment where individuals from the low-
status group have an active role in shaping the interaction,
and where their status is temporarily elevated to be equal to
that of the high-status group during the contact situation.

Fourth, the role of institutions – condition (4) above – in
facilitating positive intergroup contact should not be under-
estimated.[66] Workplaces can implement diversity training
programmes, and schools can design curriculums that include collaborative projects among students from diverse
backgrounds. In a workplace, for instance, a company might
integrate diversity training into its onboarding process. New
employees would participate in workshops that simulate various intergroup scenarios, encouraging them to engage with
and learn from the diverse perspectives of their co-workers.
This practice could be enriched with guest speakers from
different backgrounds. Such initiatives help employees understand the nuances of intergroup relations and equip them
with the skills to collaborate effectively. The attitudes and
actions of managers can significantly influence the success of
intergroup contact. When these figures actively support and
participate in diversity initiatives, it sends a strong message
about the value and importance of these efforts.

We can't discuss exposure, or any of the elements of
EMBRACE for that matter, without considering the economic and social conditions that will serve to shape how far
apart they are from one another. Economic hardship can trig-
ger intergroup conflict.[67] An increasingly unequal society can

undermine trust in public institutions and erode democratic governance, while also posing risks to geopolitical stability.[68] In societies where inequality is high, people can start questioning the fairness and effectiveness of these institutions, which can lead to a decline in civic engagement and a sense of disenfranchisement. This erosion of trust is particularly detrimental to democratic governance, as it undermines the very principles of equality and representation that democracies are built upon.

Fifth, and perhaps more importantly for making 'tolerance by design' as easy as possible, it is clear to see that most of these interventions, including the short-term ones, are resource and time intensive. If we are going to reduce beliefism in everyday life, we need to find effective ways of 'shortcutting' the requirements of contact theory. Besides rather glibly saying that we should create and seize opportunities for meaningful, cooperative interactions across different groups, what else can we do? Well, advances in technology offer some promising avenues. For example, some researchers have explored intergroup contact in virtual environments, such as online fora or virtual reality settings, where participants interact with avatars representing members of different groups.

In one case, researchers used a virtual reality (VR) environment to create conditions for intergroup contact by engaging thirty-two participants with avatars of diverse ethnicities in a virtual city.[69] The intervention ran for three weeks with periodic collaborative tasks and discussions in VR. The study concluded that participants reported a greater willingness to engage with people from different ethnic backgrounds in real life following their VR experience. Another study explored the impact of online fora on intergroup contact.[70] The researchers gathered data from 118 participants who were active in online discussion groups that were specifically designed to foster inter-ethnic dialogue. The intervention spanned six months and provided a platform for participants to discuss various topics, ranging from daily life to specific intergroup issues. The results provide suggestive early evidence that sustained participation in these fora can lead to more positive attitudes towards out-group members and a reduction in prejudicial stereotypes.

In a separate study of Jewish and Arab students using similar methods, online intergroup contact contributed to an increase in trust and a decrease in the dehumanisation of the other group.[71] Over 500 participants completed surveys before and after their involvement in a four- or eight-week programme. Follow-up surveys were conducted up to eighteen months after the programme to assess the longevity of effects. The findings revealed that prejudice levels decreased, while tendencies towards collective action, out-group knowledge and confidence in intercultural communication skills improved. These positive outcomes persisted for up to eighteen months post-programme. The study found no significant difference in the effectiveness of the programme whether it lasted for four or eight weeks.

A 2023 paper by colleagues from the LSE describes an experiment of 724 people to understand the impact of partisan (Labour or Tory) echo chambers on polarisation in England and to consider the role of differential exposure.[72] Participants were randomly assigned to either a group with only co-partisans or a group with a balanced mix of co-partisans and out-partisans. The discussions lasted about forty-five minutes, starting with a five-minute information video about immigration policy, followed by a thirty-minute group discussion facilitated by a trained moderator, and concluding with a post-treatment questionnaire. The key findings showed that participants in groups with only co-partisans became significantly more polarised after the discussion. In contrast, those in mixed groups became significantly less polarised.

As I wrap up EMBRACE and the subsection on exposure, I'm left wondering whether my own (relative and perceived) tolerance of different beliefs emanates in large part from having been exposed to a range of perspectives and people over my lifetime. Apart from a stint living in New York when I worked at Princeton University, it is true that I haven't lived anywhere other than the UK, but I have lived in several places with different degrees and kinds of ethnic diversity. And I was born in Hackney, which was a pretty diverse part of London. But more than that, as discussed at the start, I have been exposed to people of different social classes and have never moved on from my working-class friendships while at the same as working with academics who are all middle class (either by origin or assimilation). This could all be bullshit, of course, and I could just be deluding myself about my low levels of beliefism. Regardless, I am going to do more to expose myself to people who disagree with me. I might even go to a Coldplay gig. I won't.

14

EMBRACE it all

Inspired by the power of checklists to draw our attention to what should be obvious but is often overlooked, I hope that the EMBRACE checklist inspires you to incorporate its principles into your lives, clubs, organisations and institutions. First and foremost, you must be committed to being less beliefist. We must desire a world where dissent is not merely tolerated but actively embraced as a precursor for happiness, innovation and growth. We must learn to be more comfortable with ambivalence and ambiguity. The interventions designed to reduce beliefism do not sit in a vacuum. With democracy under threat around the world, not only is beliefism on the increase but the interventions designed to reduce it might prove to be less effective. So, we must retain a focus on the fundamentals of open dialogue.

With a commitment to less beliefism, the physical and virtual *environments* can be designed not only with less beliefism in mind, but with less beliefism as an objective for all those involved. *Mistakes* are seen not as an admission of weakness but rather as an indispensable component of learning. Shared objectives and values are embedded into discussion and debate to remind us of the power of *bonding*, thereby facilitating more empathetic and understanding interactions. There is respect for evidence and ethics grounded in *reason*, reminding us that not all beliefs are created equal. Proportionate *affect* is encouraged as we muddle our way through issues that may, on occasion, evoke considerable emotion. All the while, we are alert to the fact that better decisions are made from a *collection* of different people and perspectives. The ambition of a less beliefist world is much more likely when there is *exposure* to the people who see a rabbit when we see a duck.

For the elements of EMBRACE to reduce beliefism, they will obviously need to be used. So, we need to design the environment in ways that make interventions that rely on environmental factors more likely to be implemented. In the MINDSPACE checklist I developed, the M stands for *messenger*, which we have seen to be more effective than messages in shaping beliefs and behaviour. Among the most effective messengers were female hairdressers in Zimbabwe who were trained in HIV prevention and who communicated this information to their female clients while cutting their hair. The hairdressers were the perfect messengers: they were trusted, had expertise and were someone to whom the client could relate.

The most interesting question that this example raises is not so much the brilliant use of hairdressers but the processes through which hairdressers were identified as a potential messenger and then tested as such. I don't know the answer, by the way. But it beautifully illustrates how we need to be open to embracing new ways of approaching challenges like beliefism, which can sometimes feel intractable. By being less beliefist and more tolerant by design, we will generally be more open to new ideas, including those that will serve to further reduce beliefism. I hope that the EMBRACE framework can serve to fuel a virtuous cycle of evidence and innovation to help address the challenges we are facing in our personal lives, in businesses and in public policy.

To help us get further on the path to less beliefism, the book now shifts from general principles to specific issues. But before we do move on, it might be helpful to make a note of your key takeaways from EMBRACE that you could see yourself embedding into your personal and professional lives. Which element(s) resonate the most with you? Which ones lend themselves to being implemented? I've written this book because it's a purposeful experience but also because I genuinely believe we can and should be less beliefist. So, I would love to hear how you think we can take the EMBRACE framework off the pages of this book and place it at the heart of private and public debate.

Part 3

Picking Sides

Having shown how we *take* sides and the ways in which we can *break* sides, in this final part of the book, I want to consider how we *pick* sides on some important issues. Rather than bother you with loads of academic evidence on the issues, I'm going to outline the highly stylised perspectives of the two opposing sides of the argument very briefly before picking a side. I'm doing this so that you can reflect on how you feel about me when you find out that we disagree, as will surely be the case at some point. For each issue, I will also briefly discuss how an element or two of EMBRACE could be used to bring the duck and the rabbit together in ways that reduce beliefism and its spillovers. Being more specific about how EMBRACE can be applied will hopefully serve to spark further ideas of your own about how to address the current issues fuelling beliefism.

I've chosen six important and polarising topics, which according to the survey at the start of the book are the issues upon which we would most like to avoid people who disagree with us i.e., those that have the greatest likelihood of leading to beliefism. These are economic inequalities, immigration, climate change, freedom of speech, drug use and abortion. For us to engage respectfully with different beliefs, we first need to establish some of the key founding stones upon which debate can be built. A shared framework and language will reduce the likelihood of perceptions of polarisation that result from us cutting across one another with confused concepts as much as from any real difference between us.

15

The groundwork

I appreciate that there can be disagreement about what framework to adopt in the first place, but let's see how far we can get. Whatever your beliefs, you will surely agree that less overall suffering in the world is a good thing. I'll assume that you will agree with me when I say that, as a first approximation, it is incumbent on individuals, citizens, parents and policymakers to seek to reduce suffering by as much as possible. *Negative utilitarianism* views suffering in terms of how people feel.[1] A person's reports of how they are feeling may not be all that matters but they will be a useful guide to how well or badly their life is going. This means that one of the principal objectives of a civilised society should be to reduce the real suffering of real people by as much as possible. Recall from earlier that it is my contention that a legitimate belief is based on a willingness to engage with and accept the costs and benefits of its enactment, and negative utilitarianism provides us with a good starting point to assess these.

More than a feeling

There are two main ways that we may wish to depart from minimising misery.[2] The first relates to *fairness*, such that some people's misery (e.g., the worst off) might be weighted more highly than others *beyond* their individual effects. The second pertains to certain *rights* (e.g., relating to freedom of speech) that might matter *before* any concerns for individual effects. The main issues of contention of the day may seldom be framed in terms of fairness or rights, but I would suggest that they are, in fact, the main underlying sources of disagreement. To illustrate how different values surrounding fairness and rights speak directly to the substance of why people may have different views about an issue, I will consider three hotly contested issues that relate to fairness and three pertaining to rights. Before doing so, let me briefly outline how fairness and rights, respectively, go beyond and come before concerns for how people feel.

If we cared only about minimising the sum total of misery, we would care only about policies that generated the biggest bang for the buck. But few of us care only about *efficiency*. We also care about *equality* – about reducing the misery of those who are suffering the most. To illustrate this, imagine one group, X, whose happiness (or some other measure of welfare, such as health or income) is three out of ten on some scale, and another group, Y, whose happiness is one out of ten on the same scale. Assume that the groups are the same in all other morally relevant respects. Suppose for a given expenditure we could either (A) increase the happiness of group X by two or (B) increase the happiness of the group Y by one. (A) is clearly more efficient since it reduces overall suffering by twice as much but (B) narrows the gap between the two groups. Would you choose (A) or (B)? There is no right or

wrong answer to this question and so we cannot say which
outcome is best for society.

Your choice between (A) and (B) is likely to be affected
by the causes of the differences in happiness. The more the
inequality is due to 'bad choices' as compared to 'bad luck',
the less we will care about reducing it. Imagine that group
X is working hard to improve their lives and group Y is lazy.
Many of you who were initially inclined to choose (B) might
now be drawn more towards (A). There is an inequality between groups X and Y, but that does not mean it is unfair.
Even if we have very little control over what we do, there
still remains a spectrum running from chance to choice. A
gang member who gets shot in a drive-by shooting will be
seen by most people to have had marginally more control
over that outcome than a passerby, even if becoming a gang
member may involve very little agency. This is all that is required for us to have beliefs about *equity* (fairness) rather than
simply inequality. Some inequalities will be considered to be
fair. Each of us has a set of beliefs that translate into concerns
about – and meta preferences to act upon – the *size* of a given
inequality and its perceived *source*.[3]

The discussion here relates to inequalities in outcomes: in
the final distributions of happiness, health, income, etc. Many
philosophers, commentators, politicians and citizens would
rather focus on equality of opportunity.[4] The aim would be to
create a level playing field for everyone so that, to mix met-
aphors, we were all at the same starting point in the race for
riches. Any resulting inequalities in outcome could then be
considered fair in the same way as we see it as fair that there
are winners and losers in sporting competitions. Equality of
opportunity is relatively easy to operationalise at the starting
line and in the rules of sporting events, but it is almost impossible to bring it about in everyday life: even at birth there

are huge differences in the opportunities that people face. And even if equality of opportunity was possible, it may still create unacceptable inequalities in outcomes, such as income. So, I will continue to focus on the distribution of outcomes because it is often where most of the heated debates focus.

Rights place constraints on the minimisation of misery. In the language of philosophy, these are deontological concerns that matter in their own right as opposed to teleological ones that are important insofar as they generate good or bad consequences and the distribution thereof.[5] Please allow me to illustrate the difference with a provocative example. Some people assert that racism is bad because a basic human right to be treated equally is violated. Affirming rights is a morally 'strong' position to adopt. Racism is wrong. Full stop. The challenge here is that there are several basic human rights. Imagine a white person who won't ever date a black person. Should we force them to consider black partners because of a black person's basic right not to be discriminated against, or allow the white person to exercise their right to select partners based on whomever they want? How would you feel about people who choose only their own race from being banned from dating sites?

The teleological response to these questions – to any questions – is to do whatever creates the best outcome. The adoption of a deontological approach requires an exposition of which rights dominate, and why. In practice, providing evidence on the full flow of suffering over time is, to put it mildly, hugely challenging. And so, while there is a massive conceptual difference between those who adopt a deontolog- ical or a teleological perspective, any beliefism as it applies to real life issues is likely to amount to differences in beliefs about which concerns matter most. We should still be seek- ing to measure the full flow of costs and benefits wherever possible, though. It helps to ensure that we have intellectual skin in the game, remember. A morally strong position is one that recognises trade-offs rather than ignoring that the enactment of even the basic rights comes with costs, even if they are entirely justifiable.

Six points of separation

For exposition, I will discuss the issues as 'duck–rabbit problems' with two sides, although the debate will obviously be more nuanced than can be captured by an 'either/or' framing. I discussed some of the topics on my duck–rabbit podcast, recorded in 2021. I've further reflected on these issues in relation to consequences, fairness and rights, so I feel as if I am sharing more fully formed beliefs. But I'll change my mind if you can convince me otherwise, and I don't claim to have all the answers – who does? Each of the issues is discussed in about 1,500 words when ten times that still wouldn't do them justice. So please forgive my brevity for glossing over the issues. My evolving views on the six issues and the nuance therein are much less important than remaining focused on my ambitions around understanding and reducing beliefism. As we go through the issues, I would like your focus of attention to be on how you feel about the people who hold the opposite view to you (which will sometimes be me).

Let's start by seeing how your own beliefs relate to three issues of fairness: inequalities, immigration and climate. Overleaf are some statements with which you can: 1) strongly agree; 2) somewhat agree; 3) somewhat disagree; or 4) strongly disagree. The questions are deliberately simple and stylised to get at your initial and high-level reactions to the issues.

1a.   The income inequality in my country is outrageous and
      must be reduced   **1** **2** **3** **4**
1b.   Taxes should be cut because they disincentivise
      innovation and hard work   **1** **2** **3** **4**
2a.   Immigration provides enormous economic and cultural
      benefits   **1** **2** **3** **4**
2b.   Immigration causes social tensions and should be limited **1** **2** **3** **4**
3a.   Climate change is an existential crisis that we must do
      everything to mitigate   **1** **2** **3** **4**
3b.   It's too late to reverse climate change and we must learn
      to live with it   **1** **2** **3** **4**

Remember the Fab 500 from the beginning of the book?
Well, we asked them these questions too. Their answers are
below, where agree and strongly agree are put together in one
group of 'agree' and disagree and strongly disagree are put together in the other group of 'disagree'. Two things stand out.
First, there is a split across questions that is not far off fifty–fifty.
This provides further justification for discussing these issues.
Second, there is slightly more agreement than disagreement
with the statement, despite the fact that the second question in
each pair is a (sort of) reversed version of the first. This shows
that we're slightly predisposed towards agreeing with a statement rather than disagreeing with it. (You might like to keep
this in mind when framing your surveys at work, etc.)

		Agree	**Disagree**
1a.	Income inequality is outrageous	53%	47%
1b.	Taxes should be cut	54%	46%
2a.	Immigration provides benefits	55%	45%
2b.	Immigration causes social tensions	52%	48%
3a.	Climate change is an existential crisis	52%	48%
3b.	We must learn to live with climate change	55%	45%

As well as having concerns for how people feel and what's fair or not, we can also argue about whether, when and why people have certain inalienable rights, e.g., relating to freedom of speech, the right to self-determination and the right to life. Many people will say that it is fine to seek to minimise suffering but only subject to one or more of these rules/rights being satisfied. It might be worth thinking about how your own beliefs relate to these issues too. As before, below are some statements with which you can: 1) strongly agree; 2) somewhat agree; 3) somewhat disagree; and 4) strongly disagree. Again, as before, the questions are deliberately simple to get at your initial and high-level reactions to the rights.

4a.	People must be free to say whatever they like even if it really offends others	1 2 3 4
4b.	It is wrong to mock a deity, such as Allah, if many people are offended by it	1 2 3 4
5a.	People must be allowed to eat and drink, snort, smoke whatever they want	1 2 3 4
5b.	It is right that some drugs, such as cocaine and heroin, are illegal	1 2 3 4
6a.	Human life starts at conception and abortion is therefore morally wrong	1 2 3 4
6b.	A woman should have the right to terminate a pregnancy at any stage	1 2 3 4

The table overleaf shows the responses from our Fab 500. Again, there is something approximating a fifty–fifty split across the questions. Again, there is a general tendency to agree, except for the statement about life starting at conception.

		Agree	Disagree
4a.	People must be free to say whatever they like	56%	44%
4b.	It is wrong to mock a deity	54%	46%
5a.	People must be allowed to [do] whatever they want	51%	49%
5b.	It is right that some drugs are illegal	55%	45%
6a.	Human life starts at conception	47%	53%
6b.	Right to terminate a pregnancy at any stage	50%	50%

Following the discussion of each issue below, I'm going to consider how an element of EMBRACE could be used to bring the views of the duck and the rabbit together in respectful discussion. There are six issues and seven elements of EMBRACE, so for completeness one issue (it turns out to be immigration) will be related to two elements of EMBRACE. Beliefism in relation to each issue could be addressed by each element of EMBRACE. I have chosen one for illustrative purposes. You might have better ideas about which element(s) is a better 'fit' for each issue. Indeed, as noted above, in providing an illustrative example in each case, I hope to spark off better ideas about how to increase tolerance by design.

16

Fairly different

Economic inequality

Most people would agree that poverty is bad for people. It certainly makes people miserable.[6] Most of us believe that there should be a safety net below which no one should be allowed to drop. We may disagree about how low the net should be set but, in the UK at least, very few people would suggest that anyone should be allowed to starve. All governments have sought to provide effective means of getting resources to where they are needed most. Individuals also make significant private contributions to help people whose lives have fallen below certain minimum standards. There is a consensus, then, that we should look after the most vulnerable. Indeed, it has been said that the measure of a country is how it treats its poorest members. And I agree. I am proud of the fact that the UK has a minimum wage but less proud that around 4 million children live in poverty.[7]

When we think of inequality, we most often think about

economic inequality – about the distribution of wealth and income in society. Indeed, in large part our views on several issues, including immigration and climate change, will be determined by how important we consider wealth and income to be for human wellbeing, and how much we care about enduring inequalities in wealth and income. Our starting positions on these issues will also affect how we interpret evidence. Currently, there is a debate raging among economists about whether income inequality has increased over the last couple of decades.[8] Some conclude that it has, others, increasingly, that there hasn't been much change. You would think that this is a question of fact and not value, but income data are quite unreliable and so the assumptions that are made about the relationship between actual income and tax payments or self-reported income, for example, greatly affect the conclusions drawn. Surveys show people think that economic inequality is much less than it is, and that they want it to be even lower.[9]

Recall that not all inequalities are unfair. The harder you work, the more you will be rewarded by society for your efforts. The duck–rabbit problem presents itself in relation to the part that effort plays in determining success, and, consequently, how much redistribution there should be. Those on the left – who see inequality as a duck, say – argue that your position in society is largely determined for you. Many rich people are lazy, and many poor people work very hard. Redistribution from the lucky rich to the unlucky poor is the fair thing to do. Those on the right – who view the image of inequality as a rabbit – argue that your place in society is primarily determined by how hard you work. High levels of redistribution from richer to poorer people reduce the incentive to work hard, reward laziness and are unfair. 'Lefty ducks' create and curate a narrative of themselves as

defenders of compassion and poorer people, and 'righty rabbits' tell a story in which they are ambassadors for ambition
and innovation.

This is something of a false dichotomy. While I am
unashamedly a lefty duck, it is possible to believe in both
individual ambition *and* collective compassion, and to design
policies that both reward and redistribute. I am in little doubt
that how hard you work is largely determined by factors outside of your control rather than by anything you deliberately
decide upon. Why would effort be substantively different
to all the other behaviours that you have very little choice
over? The wiggle room for free will is ever decreasing as we
continue to understand more about the impact of genes, environment, and the relationship between them. Once luck is
added into the mix, there isn't much room left for volition.
Your position in society is therefore largely determined *for*
you rather than *by* you.

But it's good for us to believe we are in control even
though we might not be. Belief in free will has been shown
to be associated with better job performance.[10] A little bit
of delusion about the degree of choice we have over what
we do and how hard we work helps to get us out of bed in
the morning. While feeling like *we* have free will can often
be beneficial to us as individuals, believing that *others* act
volitionally is usually harmful to social justice. The idea
that anyone can succeed if only they work hard enough –
the 'American Dream' of liberal democracies – is born out
of wilful ignorance of systemic inequalities in the modern
world. It is entirely possible and consistent simultaneously
to encourage ambition and hard work while redistributing
resources to where they will reduce misery and suffering
the most.

As well as considering how to deal with poor people, we

also need to consider how to deal with very wealthy people, e.g., those who earn tens of millions each year. We need incentives to generate entrepreneurial activity. The super-rich people also pay about 35–40 per cent of their total income in tax and many of them do a great deal for charity (although the poorest people give more to charity as a percentage of income).[11] But the super-rich are still left with tens of millions of pounds each year, which could be used to pay for public services. As I write, Elon Musk has just been awarded a $56 billion pay deal. Fifty households in the UK own more wealth than 50 per cent of the population, i.e., more than 33 million people. Take a second for that to sink in if you didn't know it already. It's mind blowing, isn't it?

It has recently been proposed that there should be an upper limit on the amount of wealth an individual can accumulate.[12] The reasons put forward include the fact that the happiness returns from getting ever richer diminish quite quickly and could disappear completely at very high levels of wealth. A wealth limit would mean that the additional money could generate much, much more happiness for the poorest people in society. To my mind, the most compelling reason for a wealth tax would be to limit the influence that super-rich people can have on politics. I'm quite inclined to give it a go, e.g. with very high marginal tax rates kicking in at very high wealth levels; say, £1 billion. According to the 2024 *Sunday Times* Rich List, this would affect 165 people in the UK.

A wealth cap will adversely affect incentives and innovation among the super-rich around the world, and it may lead some to move countries, but they could be additionally incentivised by reputational gains through accolades and awards, which will probably do much more for their egos and happiness than more money. They could also be given a stake in how the resources taken from them would be used.

The best way for a wealth cap to work would be for several countries to agree to impose it, and perhaps to set up non-governmental bodies to allocate the resources, along the lines of the National Lottery in the UK. A single country could signal how much it cares about economic inequality by being the first mover. Would you like your country to trial a wealth cap? How do you feel about my lefty-duck values on economic inequality? How do they make you feel about *me*?

Embracing collection to reduce beliefism in relation to economic inequalities

Overall, I don't think there is anywhere near as much action taken on addressing economic inequalities as there should be. There are myriad reasons for this, but the lack of working-class people in prominent positions in society must play a part. Slow but significant progress has been made over the last few decades to increase the gender and racial diversity of the UK Parliament. At the same time, the 'representation gap' is widening by social class.[13] What is even more troubling than the decrease in working-class representation is the fact that very few people seem to care about it, as reflected by the lack of media interest. Worse than this, it feels to me like there is an implicit assumption that Parliament ought to be the preserve of those with higher levels of formal education. It's taken for granted that Parliament will contain a much higher proportion of people with a degree or equivalent than is found in the public. Research has shown that working-class MPs are more likely to support policies that tackle poverty and economic inequality.[14]

We have seen from the discussion of cognitive diversity that it's differences in ways of thinking that matter to effective decision making. But properly understanding the preferences, circumstances and constraints of the general population requires a Parliament that is as close as possible to being representative of the different preferences, circumstances and constraints in society. This requires a Parliament that is not only representative by gender and race but ideally by disability and sexual orientation too. Above all, it requires representativeness by social class. I say above all because, while very few people are assumed to aspire to being a different gender, race, etc., it is often taken for granted that working-class people would ideally want to be middle class. Some do, but many don't, and this preference needs to be properly accounted for. To be clear, most of us want a decent standard of living and respect for the contribution we make to society, but this is not the same thing as aspiring to become a banker, say, rather than a builder.

It's not just in Parliament. We need a collection of people at all levels and layers of all our organisations and institutions. We need people in senior positions who, by retaining the beliefs of the people they grew up around, can act as genuine role models for younger working-class people. And it's not just in relation to addressing economic inequalities that we need a collection of people that better reflects class differences in society. While the evidence is not indisputable, working-class people have been shown to be more collaborative and generous than their middle-class counterparts, and so having more openly working-class beliefs and behaviours in senior positions will arguably benefit productivity and wider society.[15]

So how do we do this? Well, I'm opposed to cracking this nut with the sledgehammer of quotas, so we need more subtle nudges to improve diversity in decision making relating inter alia to economic inequalities. Across a range of decision contexts, we typically witness better outcomes with more transparency than with less. We observe more volunteering and charitable giving when we can observe who's behaving well.[16] We observe less cheating and corruption when we can observe who's behaving badly.[17] So, at a minimum we should require that political parties publish the number of working-class candidates they are putting forward for election. Public companies could also be required to record the number of working-class applicants they attract at each level of the organisation.

Whenever corporate or policy decisions touch on issues of economic inequality, citizen or employee groups could be constituted to give voice to different income groups within the organisation or in society. We can advocate for greater representation of working-class people in decision-making positions by supporting grassroots movements and organisations that focus on this issue. Companies might consider partnerships with such organisations to develop leadership programmes for working-class individuals. Social media and other platforms can be used to raise awareness about the lack of representation of openly working-class individuals in positions of power. All this will be made both more likely and effective if working-class people weren't 'forced' by social expectations to become middle class in all aspects of their identity and not just that associated with the job they do. I mentioned earlier how working-class people who gain higher status jobs still face a pretty stark choice between fitting in or fucking off.

It has recently been argued by Rob Henderson that 'luxury beliefs' can serve as status symbols, reflecting a detachment from the concerns faced by 'ordinary' people.[18] Examples include extreme forms of environmentalism. At the same time as the wealthiest people in society have sought to signal their economic wealth in more subtle ways with Birkin bags and the like, they have sought to signal their 'moral' wealth through luxury beliefs that others may not be able to 'afford' if they were implemented. Luxury beliefs may have coincided with the phenomenon of 'elite overproduction'; that is, too many formally educated and overqualified people for the jobs available, e.g., as witnessed by many baristas having university degrees. For those unable to signal economic status, luxury beliefs offer an opportunity to signal superiority in other ways.[19]

Working-class people are not a homogenous group, of course. Rob Henderson and I had very different backgrounds in many ways, but both of us were unequivocally working class. We have been interested in how some of our conclusions about how to deal with poverty are quite different. But we both care greatly about reducing inequality. Some working-class people oppose further redistribution, of course, and many vote for parties that want to cut taxes on income. Many successful working-class people are against further redistribution on the grounds that their 'effort' should, rightly and handsomely, be rewarded. I recognise that I've been guilty of lumping people together into homogenous groups a bit too much here. But my point remains: debates will be enriched with a wider collection of perspectives and different experiences. If this means that support for reducing economic inequalities diminishes as a result, then I'm just going to have to make a stronger case for it.

Immigration

One contentious issue that speaks directly to concerns about fairness is immigration. In an either/or world of polarisation, you must either be an 'open-doors duck' and believe in the freedom of movement of people, or a 'restrictive rabbit' and believe in strict limits on migration. Either you see a duck and worry mostly about the economy not growing as fast as it could and, without mass migration, your country being left behind culturally as well as economically; you might also think that we have a moral duty to take migrants who want to improve their life chances by coming to the UK. Or you see a rabbit and worry mostly about jobs being taken by foreign workers, wages being pushed down and public services being overrun; you might also be concerned about the dilution of British values and behaviours.

Ideally, when discussing immigration or any other issue, we would appeal to the evidence even if it is nearly always contested. Overall, economists broadly agree that immigration into the UK has a significantly positive effect on economic growth.[20] Tax revenues increase and so more resources can be devoted to public services. But there is also evidence showing that immigrants suppress wages in certain low-skilled sectors of the economy.[21] In principle, those who lose out from immigration and globalisation *could* be more than compensated by those who gain from it, but this is typically not what happens. There are therefore legitimate reasons for opposing mass immigration on the grounds of economic inequalities among the groups of lower paid workers whose job prospects and wages are most likely to be affected by immigration. Against this background, it is unsurprising that those with higher levels of education and income have a more favourable view of immigration than those with lower levels of education and income.

In relation to its economic effects, immigration can to some large extent be seen as a perfect illustration of the efficiency–equity trade-off, and so we should discuss the economics of immigration in this way. Since the quality of debate is typically elevated with transparency, I would like to see the expected impacts of different types and levels of immigration presented and discussed by, say, income decile (each 10 per cent of the population from poorest to richest). This will hopefully serve to frame the policy discussions around how to better target immigration to the most socially impactful sectors and to ensure that the economic surplus of immigration is distributed more fairly across society.

The cultural effects of immigration are much harder to determine and, somewhat as a result, lead to quite polarised views. Migrants can bring cultural diversity and enhance our experiences of food, music and the arts, but they are also unfamiliar with some of the customs that bind us together, such as our uniquely British sense of humour. Much will depend on the degree to which immigrants integrate or separate. Those who might identify themselves as progressive liberals often imagine a multicultural society. The evidence, however, suggests that those from different countries tend to separate themselves from wider society.[22] As we discussed at length earlier on, it is a natural part of the human condition to want to be around those we consider to be like us in some important respects.

As with every issue that polarises us, it is easy to lose sight of the complexities of the situation and to instead look for lazy explanations for how those with different perspectives approach the problem. So, when white working-class people in the East End of London expressed their dismay at immigration from Bangladesh, they were labelled as racist by some progressive liberals. Some people are racist, of course, but there was nothing inherently racist about the specific concern that the allocation of social housing wasn't taking full account of how long a family had lived in the neighbourhood. When social housing was allocated principally according to family size, larger Bangladeshi families might leapfrog white working-class families who had lived in the area for generations. As someone whose family came from the East End for several generations, I think it's only fair that how long someone has lived in an area should be an important consideration in the allocation of social housing.[23]

Indeed, concerns for fairness run through my approach to any issue, and how I would ask that we approach immigration. In this way, I reckon we can find much more of a consensus – and certainly less beliefism – than exists at present. Most of us would think it is fair to allow into the country people who will make a net contribution to society. Most of us would agree that it is then fair to compensate those who lose out from immigration through the economic gains of people coming to the UK. Most of us would also agree that it is right and proper to ask immigrants quickly to learn to speak English, fully to abide by UK laws and customs, and generally to integrate into British society and culture. Most of us would agree that immigrants add significantly to our culture.

None of this strikes me as especially controversial, or at least it shouldn't be. And yet both the duck and the rabbit in the debate about immigration often adopt language that I find distasteful and disrespectful of those who favour immigration and those who have legitimate concerns about it. We need to take the rhetoric out of the debate. But if I was forced to choose between duck or rabbit, I would choose to be the restrictive rabbit and not an open-doors duck. How does that make you feel about me? I would come down this way if forced to pick a side primarily because of where we are at the present time. About two decades ago, less than one in ten people in the UK was non-white. Currently it is more than one in five and rising.[24] This rapid increase over a relatively short time is not in itself problematic. But there are now pockets of the country where English is a second language. This prevents reasonable dialogue – and laughter and general small talk – across groups.

I would contend that, after prioritising diversity over the last couple of decades, it's time to prioritise inclusion for a while. Quite rightly, priorities ebb and flow over time, partly as political winds change but also substantively in response to changing circumstances. One thing is for sure, politicians need to come much closer to doing what they say they will. Immigration levels have been much higher under successive governments than predicted and no government in the UK over the last twenty years has managed to reduce immigration despite saying they would.[25] There must be a shift in Europe, and perhaps in the US too, towards transparent and effective immigration policies that reduce reliance on low-wage labour, and which instead focus on high-skilled immigrants. This is the most effective way to counter the rise of right-wing populism, which has become more prominent over the last decade or so.

If we are going to place relatively greater emphasis on inclusion, then we will need to face up to one very significant change: the rapid decline in the fertility rate. A fertility rate of 2.1 is required for population stability. The UK's is currently 1.5 and falling. This means that the ratio of working-age people to retired people is falling, placing an ever-increasing burden on the former to support the latter. One way to address this is through immigration from countries with much higher fertility rates, such as those in Sub-Saharan Africa. There is little doubt that we will need to do this to some extent and so any emphasis on inclusion must grapple with this balancing act. Thankfully, notwithstanding recent challenges from the pace of immigration, the UK's long and very proud record of coping with immigration will stand it in good stead here.

To limit the reliance on immigration, though, we will need to consider a substantial overhaul of the welfare system to ease the burden on working-age adults. This should include raising the retirement age. It is worth noting that when 'the old-age pension' was first introduced in the UK in 1908 for those aged over seventy, it was way above the average life expectancy of around fifty. It strikes me that a significant increase in the retirement age is at least as good a policy option as mass immigration in response to falling fertility rates. If people had to work for longer, there would be greater demand from workers for their jobs to feel purposeful rather than, as is the case currently, many people counting down towards their retirement – and a retirement which, in reality, frequently turns out to be less pleasurable than predicted. You might disagree, but there are no easy choices, and so we need to flush out the underlying values that should underpin the kind of society we want.

Embracing environment and bonding to reduce beliefism in relation to immigration

Ethically, so far as immigration is concerned, a lot will turn on how we define the in- and out-groups of priority. If we think of everyone on the planet as the in-group with no out-group, then the welfare of immigrants should be placed entirely alongside that of residents. This would mean that mass immigration would be much more attractive because immigrants typically have lower levels of income. But we are a world of nation states, with geographic and political borders. In democracies and autocracies alike, the principal concerns of both elected and unelected politicians are for the

residents of their own country. A politician can favour their
constituents as an MP, but they are responsible for the country as a minister. A national politician can favour their own
country's residents but someone working at an international
aid agency should look at suffering anywhere.

The degree of (im)partiality in the perspective we adopt
will therefore depend on our specific roles in the environments within which we act. It is legitimate for me to put my
kids first as a parent but not if I was a coach of their sports
team, where my own kids should be treated just like any other
team member. I care greatly about poor people elsewhere in
the world, and we must do more than we are presently to
assist them. But, as a British national, I also care more about
poor people in the UK. So, one way to reduce beliefism and
its associated spillovers in any context, but perhaps especially
in the context of immigration, is to ask people to wear different decision-making hats.

This is akin to perspective taking discussed earlier, whereby
constructive framing techniques can reduce polarisation.[26]
Recall that active listening is the critical step in the process.
We need to fully engage with different vantage points on
immigration and with the complexity of the issue. Given its
complexity, humility and curiosity are both vital ingredients
of how we approach immigration and inter alia the difficult
balancing act between diversity and inclusion. You could
consider cultivating a personal space to engage in 'difficult'
discussions, like quiet coffee shops or during peaceful walks
in nature with friends. The general framing of an issue is
crucial to how it is perceived by the public, and especially so
in relation to migration.[27] For the reasons discussed above,
the issue should be framed in the wider economic context
and consequences of fertility rates and replacement ratios, as
well as the cultural consequences of the pace of immigration.

Rather than driving a wedge between new and old immigrants (we were all immigrants at some point[28]), we should seek to identify ways to emphasise the shared hopes, goals and life experiences that transcend any divide. This creates bonding experiences that make it safer to have divergent beliefs. You could participate in community groups or activities that bring together people from diverse backgrounds. This could be a sports team, a book club, a choir or local community service group. It could also involve much more informal interactions in coffee shops and bars. Talking about sport and music are great bonding experiences. As a long-suffering West Ham fan, it's easy to bring self-deprecating humour into the conversation at any stage, which we have seen is a great way to break down barriers and to bond.

Companies should conduct audits of their physical and cultural environments to identify and mitigate any factors that contribute towards beliefism. Reevaluating organisational hierarchies and practices, such as hiring and promotion criteria, can help identify and correct implicit biases that disadvantage certain groups. Companies could support their diverse range of employees, including any new immigrants, in bonding within the organisation. They could facilitate opportunities for dialogue where employees share personal stories and find commonalities. Businesses can organise regular team-building activities, for example, that encourage employees to share their backgrounds and personal stories in a safe and supportive setting. In situations where conflicts arise, introducing a neutral mediator who is skilled in conflict resolution can be beneficial. This mediator can help to reframe contentious issues by using inclusive language, such as substituting 'but' with 'and' to acknowledge and validate multiple viewpoints, and to serve as a reminder of shared goals and ambitions.

There are plenty of options for governments to reduce beliefism about immigration by design. They could implement educational campaigns highlighting the common dreams immigrants and citizens have for their families. They could support initiatives where immigrants and locals work together on community projects/causes. They could fund cross-cultural events celebrating the diverse traditions that make up the national fabric. They could organise regular inter-departmental workshops that not only focus on policy work but also include activities designed to enhance inter-personal relations and understanding among policymakers. These could involve collaborative problem-solving challenges that require mixed teams to devise solutions to hypothetical scenarios in immigration policy, thereby fostering a sense of unity and shared purpose. Crucially, politicians should always be alert to the language they use when discussing immigration.

Climate change

Another powerful illustration of beliefism is in relation to climate change. It is an issue that goes beyond weighing different lifetimes at any one moment in time to consider wellbeing across the generations. Most of us acknowledge that the world faces a significant challenge from human-made climate change, but there is considerable disagreement about how far we are willing to go in dealing with it, and what other objectives of human wellbeing we are willing to trade off in dealing with it. Our best estimates on the potential economic costs of a 1 degree rise in temperature vary between around 2 and 12 per cent loss in global GDP. While all methods face significant challenges and there are

too many uncertain parameters and missing variables reliably to estimate the costs of climate change, there is a broad
consensus that climate change comes with greater costs than
initially imagined.[29]

The key debate boils down to the conditions under which,
and the extent to which, we should pursue *mitigation* policies
as compared to *adaptation* measures. 'Mitigation ducks' seek to
address the causes of climate change and to limit CO_2 emissions in a time frame that allows ecosystems to adapt. The use
of renewable energies is a good example. On the other hand,
'adaptation rabbits' argue for adjusting to climate change by
reducing our vulnerability to its harmful effects. Examples
would be flood defences, developing drought-resistant crops
to secure food supplies, and redesigning urban areas to better
cope with heatwaves. Any sensible and sustainable attempts to
deal with climate change will clearly involve a combination
of the two approaches. We can develop new technologies to
slow down climate change, while at the same time preparing
to cope with the consequences of change. And those who
favour nuclear energy can do so on the grounds of mitigation
or adaptation.

In most instances, though, the resources committed to
mitigation cannot also be committed to adaptation, and so
the debate has polarised into ducks who want to stop climate
change as quickly as possible and rabbits who want to reduce
its harms more slowly. Just Stop Oil (JSO) is perhaps the best
representation of the former view in the UK. JSO's aim is
to end new fossil fuel licensing and production. It seeks to
persuade the government through nonviolent civil disobedience designed to draw attention to its cause. I have a lot
of sympathy with JSO. Fossil fuel licences slow down the
incentives to move to renewables, which are increasingly a lot
less expensive than predicted. Moreover, we saw earlier how

much narratives matter to determining policy and driving human behaviour, and licences also signal to individuals and institutions that there is less urgency to engage in behaviours that would serve to slow down climate change. They also do not send a very good signal to developing countries to slow their extraction of fossil fuels.

I have a lot less sympathy with JSO's actions than I do with their ambitions. Causing disruption is increasingly the main aim of their activities rather than a byproduct of their protests. I think this is a morally relevant distinction and the degree to which you think it is legitimate will largely depend on your views about how the protests will impact upon government policy. On balance, I think that they will be counterproductive as people focus on the actions and not the aims. This would seem to be happening if the harsh sentences that were handed down in July 2024 to five JSO protestors who planned to cause disruption on a major traffic route in the UK are anything to go by. It has been interesting to witness the polarising debate about the proportionality of those sentences being driven by beliefs about climate change. In principle, these are different issues. Quite aside from the stated aims of the protests, I think that seeking to cause disruption goes beyond the provisions of freedom of speech and should be punished – but nowhere near to the tune of a five-year stretch.

Notwithstanding the specifics of JSO, protest groups and advocacy might be more effective in limiting climate change than individual behaviour change.[30] They have the potential to change government policy in much more significant ways than even great swathes of the population changing their consumption behaviour. Collective and individual action are not mutually exclusive, of course, but they might push against one another if people engage in *permitting spillovers*.

This is where engaging in one 'good' behaviour crowds out another 'good' one. If we think we are doing our bit for the environment by recycling, say, we may permit ourselves to ignore getting involved in advocacy because we are already doing our bit. Permitting spillovers are pervasive, and so it's surprising this hasn't been discussed more here.[31]

Permitting spillovers are less likely to apply at the international level. The UK doing its bit to reduce CO_2 emissions is hardly going to spill over into us doing less to cajole other countries to act. Quite the opposite, in fact. If we are doing our bit, then this will *promote* activities to get other countries to do likewise. It is also true, of course, that the UK contributes less than 1 per cent to global CO_2 emissions, so most of the effective strategies we could employ will be those that make it more likely that other countries act. And we surely make action more likely by doing our bit rather than by sitting back and saying, 'Oh, we only contribute a tiny fraction to global CO_2 so who cares what we do?' Climate change is a collective action problem, and it requires global action, led by those countries (like the UK) who have benefited most from historically high emission levels.

Ultimately, climate change, like any other issue, requires that we better navigate our way through the various trade-offs. The substantive trade-off is between the welfare of those living today and those who will be born tomorrow. I recognise that things are not as straightforward as this. What we do about human welfare and its distribution today will affect the trade-offs we make in the future and, critically, climate change, like most phenomena, affects the poorest people the most. But as I have argued throughout, it sometimes makes the issue more tractable and less polarising if we can boil it down to the fundamental trade-offs involved. Most people care much more about the poor people of today than the poor people of tomorrow, and quite rightly so. The effects of climate change and any policies that seek to reduce its harms should, first and foremost, consider those who are already alive.

On balance, I am an adaptation rabbit. Does this surprise you; annoy or please you? Perhaps you don't care what I think. As a principle of justice, I would contend that the poorest people of today should not be asked to make too many sacrifices for the hypothetical people of tomorrow. Tomorrow, quite literally, is another day, whereas today's misery is real and tangible. If a consequence of this is that the world's population will need to shrink, for example, then so be it.[32] The argument is supported by research suggesting that smaller populations can adapt more effectively to climate change by reducing per capita resource consumption,[33] alleviating pressure on ecosystems, improving resource availability, and enhancing overall quality of life. We have a much greater moral obligation to address current suffering over prospective harms.[34] Climate change is increasingly affecting current generations, and this makes addressing those harms a moral imperative. But I think it leads mostly to adaptation policies.

Intergenerational discount rates are a critical component of public policy analysis, shaping decisions that affect future generations, such as climate policy, infrastructure investment and conservation efforts. These rates quantify how current decision makers value future benefits and costs. Empirical studies on intergenerational discount rates have provided a range of values, reflecting diverse public and expert opinions. For instance, the Stern Review on the Economics of Climate Change advocated for a near-zero discount rate, which means great regard for future generations.[35] Contrastingly, more conventional economic approaches often suggest discount rates between 3 and 5 per cent, based on market interest rates and time preference data, implying a higher weight to present-day benefits. The tricky challenge lies in balancing the ethical imperative to consider future generations with the practical considerations of current societal needs.

Utilitarianism based on total happiness or suffering has always struck me as rather odd. Assuming that life is generally worth living, it leads to the conclusion that population growth is a good thing. I think that it is much better to focus on average welfare, whereby population growth is a good thing only if people will be better off, on average, than those already alive. Climate change is already making many places very uncomfortable to live. I am willing to accept that some nations will shrink. As noted under the discussion of immigration, this will require a radical revision to our economic models and to welfare systems, which are predicated on birth rates being at least as high as death rates so that younger people can generate economic growth and support older people in later life. A significant increase in the retirement age once again strikes me as a much better option than increasing population size. Do you agree? I hope you don't hate me if you disagree.

Embracing reason to reduce beliefism in relation to climate change

While there are still those who deny human-made climate change, they represent an ever diminishing and less vocal minority. The evidence on how our actions are increasing global temperatures has become more compelling and widely accepted. This shows that reason can sometimes win out, slowly but surely. We saw earlier that a jury or assembly of the public is one way of engaging citizens in thoughtful, evidence-based deliberation of an issue. As we muddle our way through how to balance the needs of current and future generations, it strikes me that we should be making more use of deliberative approaches. An 'informed' public will also be ideal messengers for communicating the challenges faced by climate change to the wider population.

In fact, a citizens' Climate Assembly (CA) to debate climate change and to provide recommendations to government took place in the UK in 2020.[36] The 108 members of the assembly were representative of the UK population in terms of: age, gender, ethnicity, educational level, where in the UK they live, whether they live in an urban or a rural area, and their level of concern about climate change. By and large, the assembly reached what most people would consider to be sensible conclusions, essentially recognising both the duck and the rabbit in the climate change image. It wanted to mitigate while at the same adapting, and its recommendations were alert to the burden borne by poorer people. For example, assembly members recommended a future that minimises restrictions on travel and lifestyles, placing the emphasis on shifting to electric vehicles and improving public transport, rather than on large reductions in car use.

Many environmentalists were very critical of the CA for not having any real decision-making powers. But while citizens' assemblies can serve an important function in advising, they will always lack the legitimacy to make decisions. Criticisms were also raised about the CA not being asked to consider whether the UK's aim of reaching net zero by 2050 should be brought forward. This is a fair point, perhaps, but I suspect that they would have been critical of any conclusions that involved trade-offs between addressing climate change and tackling other economic challenges. There are, of course, plenty of environmentalists who have intellectual skin in the game by outlining the costs and benefits of different courses of action, but several write as if addressing climate change is the *only* thing that matters.[37]

One thing is for sure in relation to the role of reason, climate change communication certainly needs to be more nuanced in its presentation of information so that we can be more nuanced in our response. Climate scientist Patrick T. Brown argues that the narrative of climate change as the sole cause of wildfires has been overamplified, overshadowing other significant factors, such as forest management.[38] His critique extends to prestigious journals like *Nature*, which favour a particular storyline that aligns with the prevailing consensus on climate change impacts. This trend, he argues, stems from the intense pressure on researchers to publish in high-profile journals, which leads to groupthink raising its ugly head, as studies are tailored to fit the expectations of journal editors and reviewers. Brown advocates a more balanced exploration of climate change that includes adaptation strategies. His views have not gone uncontested[39] but this serves to remind us that we need legitimate institutions and processes through which to bring together diverse opinions.

It's essential that decision making surrounding climate change is driven by solid data and measurable impacts, rather than relying on preconceptions or anecdotal evidence. This involves gathering comprehensive, high-quality data on environmental impacts, which should then be made accessible and understandable to all stakeholders, including citizens, businesses and policymakers. To deepen personal understanding and engage more critically with climate issues, individuals can take the initiative to educate themselves through various media. Reading books, watching documentaries and following thought leaders who present diverse perspectives on how to address climate change can all enrich our understanding. Engaging in debates or discussions, especially with those who hold opposing views, is another vital way to appreciate the complexity of climate issues and refine our own views.

As elsewhere, transparency is crucial in these efforts. For instance, regulations could be implemented requiring companies publicly to disclose their environmental footprints in a format that is easily interpretable by the general public. Additionally, toolkits designed to help collect and analyse environmental data can be provided. These might include templates for surveying public opinion on climate issues, methods for gathering demographic data relevant to environmental impact, and case studies that demonstrate the tangible outcomes of various climate policies. To further empower individuals and organisations to make informed decisions, training programmes for employees could be developed by government agencies to enhance skills for evidence-based decision making, covering such topics as critical thinking and how to evaluate data from different sources.

17

Reserving the right to disagree

Freedom of speech

Some people – let's call them the 'permitting ducks' – will hold freedom of speech to be a right. I'm one of those ducks. I find picking a side on this issue about as easy as I do about picking a side on economic inequalities. But rights also come with responsibilities. The classic example is that I would get into legal and social trouble if I shouted 'fire' in a crowded space and people got injured from panicking and rushing towards an exit. As with several issues, herein lies a difficult balancing act between, on the one hand, defending a right and, on the other hand, being alert to the harms exercising that right might have. It has been illegal for a few decades now to say something that results in physical harm.[40] Most people would think that these are legitimate grounds for curtailing freedom of speech.

I grew up, politically at least, in the 1980s during the Cold War when those living behind the 'Iron Curtain' in eastern

Europe were heavily constrained in what they were able to say and do. I daresay I was shaped by this to think that freedom of speech was something to be treasured and fought for. I also grew up around the time that the National Front and then the British National Party (BNP), both racist organisations, held marches to protest at immigration and in favour of keeping Britain white (whatever the fuck that means). It was much more acceptable to air racist views a couple of decades ago, let alone in the 1980s, than it is now. I have seen how the arguments of the racists have been dismantled through exposure rather than by censure. Many of you may remember the appearance of Nick Griffin, the leader of the BNP at that time, on *Question Time*.[41] His arguments were dismantled and, thankfully, the BNP has never really recovered.

For the past decade in the UK, 'hate speech' relating to psychological harm has been a criminal offence. It is now a hate crime if the offender demonstrated hostility based on race, religion, disability, sexual orientation or transgender identity. It probably goes without saying, even if you are unfamiliar with the UK context, that this law is not without its problems, especially as it relates to definition and the role of context. There is no legal definition of hostility, so the Crown Prosecution Service uses 'the everyday understanding of the word which includes ill-will, spite, contempt, prejudice, unfriendliness, antagonism, resentment and dislike'. You can see how broad and open to interpretation this is. There have certainly been some arrests for hate crime that can, at best, be described as silly, including a sixteen-year-old autistic girl who was arrested for homophobia when she said that a police officer 'looked like her lesbian nana' (her nan is indeed a lesbian).[42]

Restrictions on freedom of speech can be quite subtle, and perceptions matter. In the UK, about three in five Britons

have at times refrained from expressing their political or
social views due to fear of judgement or negative responses.[43]
The sentiment of self-censorship is more common among
those holding views that would be considered as less progressive on social issues. When it comes to balancing free speech
with preventing offensive or hateful speech, Britons are split;
38 per cent prioritise protecting free speech, while 43 per
cent prioritise protecting against offensive or hateful speech.
There are some age and gender differences here with slightly
more support for freedom of speech among older people and
men. The US has a long and strong history of opposition to
government censorship, but millennials are more equivocal,
with about 40 per cent in favour of the government being
able to prevent people from making statements offensive to
minority groups (compared to 15 per cent of the boomer
generation).[44]

These days, there would certainly appear to be more
people who are in favour of ostracising those who air views
that are considered offensive or unacceptable. Let's call those
in favour of 'cancelling' people for offensive views the 'censorious rabbits'. I don't wish this to sound as harsh as it might,
but I couldn't think of a better label for those who, sometimes
quite legitimately, wish to place constraints on what people
are free to say. We love labels because it allows us to provide
some order and structure to an otherwise complex and cha-
otic world, but the language and framing of those labels is of
course critical to how they are perceived. Some of you might
embrace being called censorious and others less so, but my
use of the word is simply to describe those who would like
to place some restrictions on what people are allowed to say
beyond constraints relating to physical harms.

I ain't no rabbit. I am committed to freedom of speech even
when it causes offence. So, the proliferation of police powers

with hate-crime laws concerns me. How do you feel about those laws, and about me? It concerns me that religions are using being offended to restrict being mocked and criticised. It concerns me that major tech platforms like YouTube, Facebook and Twitter/X have been criticised for banning or deplatforming certain individuals or groups based on their views. And given my job, it especially concerns me that academic speakers have been disinvited or met with aggressive protests on campus because of their views. Academics should discuss and dissent. Recall that having a good argument was one of the reasons I became an academic. I'm not sure that reason would hold today, and so I might no longer choose an academic path if I was thirty years younger. Sadly – to steal a phrase from the brilliant *Douglas Is Cancelled* – we are closer to a world of 'net zero cognitive content' in what academics say than we are to net zero carbon emissions.[45]

My views on freedom of speech could be seen to represent a departure from a negative utilitarian calculus, which would see the suffering caused by offence as a harm that could be mitigated by restrictions on what can be said. But we need to consider all the ripple effects of censure and not just its initial splash. Curtailing free speech can prevent bad ideas from being properly dismissed and it could create further divisions in society if certain groups are pushed underground. It can stifle new ideas, and limit creativity and innovation. Exposure to a variety of viewpoints is crucial for intellectual growth, and shielding students from controversial or offensive ideas can result in increased sensitivity and a reduced ability to engage in critical thinking.[46] I am willing to accept some harms so that the full benefits from freedom of speech can be realised.

You can make a different judgement call, of course, but you must accept that there will be unintended harms following from a well-intentioned attempt to protect the sensitivities of given groups. Just as I am required to make a case for why, in the longer run, freedom of speech is beneficial to society, those who want to curtail free speech must be required to make a clear case for why the benefits are worth the cost. They must also provide clear criteria on what kinds of offence are allowed, to whom, and when, just as most of us would think it reasonable to sanction someone who deliberately lies by shouting fire in a crowded space. The deliberate lie is what is relevant here, and my limits on freedom of speech would not go much beyond deliberately speaking untruths.

Beyond this, we must all be alert to freedom of speech being used to bully people. We must certainly do more to understand the experiences and beliefs that cause people to have different views about rights and responsibilities. Moreover, we should of course exercise our freedom of speech judicially. We should think before we speak, and properly consider the harm that what we are about to say might potentially cause. When we fail to consider the impact we have, it is right that there is social sanction for offending someone unnecessarily. Perhaps the real issue here is the vilification of people who disagree with us. This brings us right back to beliefism. We must be allowed to cause some offence some of the time as we muddle our way through the pursuance of new ideas and approaches that might reduce overall suffering in the longer term. I'm an inveterate optimist, at least according to the late and great Danny Kahneman, and I think that good arguments will beat bad ones from flushing out and not from cancelling out.

Embracing mistakes to reduce beliefism in relation to freedom of speech

My belief in freedom of speech is predicated on a belief that most people who cause offence do not mean to. I know that might sound a bit naive, but I think it's a good starting point and, by itself, would reduce beliefism. I seek to challenge and provoke, but only ever in ways that will serve to reduce overall suffering into the longer term. I never (OK, well, rarely) seek to piss people off for the sake of it, and most other people don't either. If I piss you off, I'll say sorry and, where possible, seek to mitigate any harm caused. And I would hope that you would accept my apology. You don't have to, of course, but I would not expect to be censured in any way. An apology should count for something quite significant in how we judge human behaviour. I'm not talking about empty claims like 'I didn't mean it' but rather a genuine apology coupled with actions that seek to put right any wrongs. Creating environments that not only allow us to fuck up from time to time but also to be afforded the opportunity to apologise is vital for the effective enactment of the right to free speech.

One of my best mates grew up, as I did, at a time when calling women 'birds' was the norm (I never conformed to that norm as it has always struck me as a sexist word). He was still using it until a year or so ago when I decided to pick him up on it. He was pleased that I did, and he has not used the word again (at least not around me). We are becoming more progressive (in a good way) in our language without having to introduce laws that could end up causing a backlash and do more harm than good. Nothing is ever purely duck or rabbit, and, yes, context matters. Nowhere does context matter more than in judging what we say. We can't know whether something is offensive, racist, or whatever, without knowing the context. We must not jump to conclusions. My mate never meant any offence by calling women birds but appreciated that, unintentionally, he might.

We don't seem to be doing very well at any of this.

Consider the recent experience of the musician Róisín Murphy.[47] In 2023, she was effectively removed from the BBC 6 Music lineup (though the BBC denies this) for posting on Facebook that she was concerned about the impact of puberty blockers on young people. Regardless of whether you see her views as transphobic, there is a much more important aspect to this story. Following the backlash, Róisín quickly apologised for the hurt that her comments had caused some people, acknowledged that she was unsuitable for the discourse around the issue, and made clear that she was now bowing out of the conversation. This appeared to have little effect on how she was treated. We must be allowed to make mistakes. You might think that Róisín was making some valid points, or you might have been outraged by what she said. But the point is that she apologised. And that should have put a stop to her vilification.

We need to give someone who has offended us the time to apologise, and this means not wading in immediately. We must show the requisite humility to recognise that we can sometimes be quite clumsy also. It is incumbent on us all to attempt to develop a more forgiving attitude by engaging in self-reflection and considering the full circumstances before reacting publicly to perceived offences. Reflect on your conversations to identify moments where you might have been dismissive or overly critical of differing views in ways that shut down the conversation. Such approaches not only facilitate less beliefism but also protect the fundamental principles of free speech and constructive discourse. I know I have been trying to make a case for less beliefism made easy, but we need to be committed to reducing beliefism in the first place, and this can sometimes be challenging for us.

We have seen how it is possible to embed learning from mistakes into workplaces, and the same set of 'tools' can be applied in relation to freedom of speech. For example, by implementing a 'no-blame' policy where mistakes are seen as opportunities for learning alongside promoting psychological safety that fosters a culture where employees feel safe to voice their opinions. This policy would distinguish between unintentional errors and deliberate harm, focusing on the former as opportunities for growth rather than grounds for punishment. To further support a positive communication environment, companies should set up robust feedback mechanisms where employees can anonymously share their experiences and suggestions for improving communication practices.

Our politicians can be asked to set a much better example in how they deal with being offended. Every time there is a misstep by a politician across the aisle, there will be an outcry for the offender to resign. The response is frequently disproportionate to what has been said. So, how about the media say to the main political parties that they have, say, two 'resign requests' a year? Yeah, I know there are all sorts of problems with this, but would it be any worse than the state we're in? We need to think of creative ways to incentivise politicians to have robust and respectful discussions, e.g., through public recognition and greater use of awards (some of which exist already[48]) for engaging in effective conflict resolution. The media are not blameless here. They should be asked – and incentivised – to consider more robustly how much they are stoking an issue rather than merely reporting on it. Media outlets might be granted access to exclusive interviews or insights from political figures based on their adherence to ethical reporting standards that prioritise seriousness over sensationalism.

The right to self-determination

In a brilliant 1989 stand-up comedy sketch, used in the equally brilliant 1999 film *Human Traffic*, the late Bill Hicks said, 'I have taken drugs before . . . and I had a real good time.' Lots of people experience drugs in this way. Lots of people get 'runner's high' after intense exercise. Many people will view the drug taking as a vice and the exercise as virtuous. You might have that initial reaction. This might still be what you think once you have reflected upon it (though I suspect not quite so strongly). If you can cast your mind back as far as the beginning of this book, you will recall that people with views that are different to ours about drugs are the people that we want to most avoid by some considerable extent. What exactly is it that makes many of us view one category of leisure pursuit as bad and another as good? What is it that makes many people support laws that not only proscribe certain drug-related highs but can put people in prison for breaking them?

For the purposes of exposition, let us compare MDMA with 10K runs and assume that each is 'taken' once a month for recreational purposes. Perhaps we are more concerned about other people's health than we are about their happiness? If MDMA causes lower life expectancies and worse life experiences than running 10K, then there might be grounds for making it illegal. But I reckon that recreational use of MDMA is at least as healthy for us as running. There are significant mental health benefits that come from the consumption of MDMA (it was originally used in therapy in the US in the 1980s) just as there are emotional highs from running.[49] MDMA is associated with come downs but, at the same time, I bet you can't find anyone who runs long distances whose knees aren't shot to bits. Despite this, I have no desire to stop people running stupid distances.

I am very much a 'libertarian duck' as opposed to a 'paternalistic rabbit' when it comes to drug laws. How do you feel about me now? Even if drugs did cause more health harms, it strikes me as sadistically paternalistic to force people to be healthy at the expense of being happy. We each have different values, priorities and risk tolerances, and the state, by and large, lets us muddle through in most domains of life apart from drug taking. Indeed, there are probably better paternalistic grounds for intervening in the types of relationships we have than in the drugs we take. What might be a fulfilling and meaningful experience for one person could be seen as reckless or unnecessary by another. By imposing a singular view of what's 'good' or 'safe' for everyone, paternalistic policies stifle individuality, personal growth and the pursuit of happiness. It's much better to inform than to insist.

Perhaps we consider drugs to be more addictive than running? Well, it's an open question about whether someone who takes MDMA monthly is any more addicted than a monthly 10K runner. But so what, even if they are both addicted? They may still judge that the benefits from their monthly pursuits outweigh the costs from their addiction. Perhaps we think that drug users are less productive than runners? This is an open question too. MDMA can enhance creativity of thought in ways that a runner's high never can. And besides, society has celebrated the (economic) performance-enhancing effects of some drugs, like caffeine, sugar[50] and alcohol,[51] for centuries.

Perhaps there is something wrong with happiness gained from chemical enhancement? Sometimes a distinction is made between 'natural' and 'unnatural' ways of improving mental and physical health. Many people will think it's OK for athletes to train at altitude but not to take steroids. The trouble is that the distinction between natural and unnatural is very blurred. Many runners will take legal stimulants to help them run faster, for example, and what is and what is not on the list of banned substances changes. More significantly, you'd be hard pressed to find many people who were against helping to make people happier by using chemicals for physical and mental pain relief. It's all a bit baffling.

Judgements about social class undoubtedly play a part. We judge people badly who engage in health-related behaviours that are much more prominent among working-class people, such as illegal drug use and the overconsumption of food. But unless we are causing harm to others and unless it can be clearly shown that we are categorically harming ourselves in ways that we would never agree to if we had more and better information, then we should be left to crack on with getting high in whatever ways we want. Everything in life is a trade-off, and we should be allowed to decide whether the health and other costs of taking drugs (or running or whatever) are a price worth paying for the happiness and other benefits that come from that choice.

Rarely is an issue completely duck or rabbit and, even as a pretty hardcore libertarian duck, I recognise that we can't be left alone to do literally whatever we want. We don't let kids drink alcohol and we ban them from using their addiction devices (their phones) in the classroom. As our brains are developing all the way through to our mid-twenties, there are good grounds for limiting access to drugs and alcohol until this age. I'm a libertarian for adults but quite paternalistic in relation to children and young adults. Most of my friends who have had healthy relationships with drugs started their 'drugs careers' in their mid-twenties. On balance, I think the UK government's recent attempts to ban cigarettes for each new cohort of sixteen-year-olds is a good idea – but better still to my mind would have been to incrementally ban smoking until the age of, say, twenty-five.

The impact of our actions on others must also be properly accounted for. It's one thing taking risks with your health when you're a twenty-five-year-old single man, it's quite another when you're a thirty-five-year-old father of two young kids. When someone becomes a parent, they become responsible for someone who can't be held responsible for themselves. The trade-offs a parent makes about the costs and benefits of their actions should therefore change – and the legal and social consequences of those trade-offs can legitimately change too. Rights come with responsibilities and those responsibilities change through the life course. There has been far too little discussion of this in policy and ethical discussions, and there should be much more.

If we do decriminalise MDMA and other drugs, they should be placed within strongly regulated markets. Access should be tightly controlled and restricted to specific times and places. Once the crime gangs are taken out of the market, so much as this is possible, governments could also use price as a rationing device for drugs, in the same way as they do (and could do more) for alcohol. They can also regulate the strength of the drugs in the same way as food companies are restricted in the amount of salt and sugar they put in food. Other drugs, such as cocaine and heroin, will require much stronger regulation. Arguably, given its impact on accidents and violent incidents, we should regulate alcohol much more than currently.

But let's be clear. The human condition has long sought to find ways to get high. We must get over ourselves about this and create environments and drug laws that allow us to get as high as we like in as safe and grounded a way as possible. There is no one-size-fits-all drug and there can't be a one-size-fits-all drugs policy, paternalistic or otherwise. The move towards decriminalisation should be a slow and cautious one, with evidence on costs and benefits gathered at all stages along the way. We must do more to accommodate individual differences. You might prefer MDMA or a glass of wine – or a long-distance run (or, indeed, all of these things, although I suggest the drugs come after the run). As Carl Hart writes in his book *Drug Use for Grown-ups* – and I paraphrase and grossly simplify a lot here, of course – each to their own.[52] But ultimately, in the words of Talk Talk, 'It's my life, don't you forget'.

Embracing affect to reduce beliefism in relation to the right to self-determination

Most of our judgements, including those relating to how others behave, come from fast and emotional (system 1) reactions rather than slow (system 2) deliberations. In *Happy Ever After*, I show how we seek to rationalise and justify our initial aversive reactions to people who are obese by using spurious logic, e.g., relating to the healthcare costs of obesity.[53] This is not to say that the harms of obesity should be ignored but rather that they are almost certainly overstated because of the emotional reactions against it. Obesity, just like any other issue, should be approached through a better understanding of not only the evidence, and reasons why and the extent to which it matters, but also the bases upon which our emotional reactions to it shape our assessments of the evidence.

While we're on the subject of obesity, there is now a class of highly effective weight-loss drugs that help to make people feel satiated sooner so that they eat less.[54] Some people will consider taking the drug to be 'cheating' because it is not 'natural' and does not require effort and sacrifice to lose weight.

Gluttony is a sin, after all, and society expects us pay for our sins through penance and not to be absolved by pharmaceuticals. But demand for the drugs is very high and they are quickly becoming an accepted path towards thinness. This shows that beliefs can change quite quickly, especially when the wellbeing gains are high. It's an open question about how the new drugs for obesity will affect beliefism and its spillovers. Obese women have consistently been discriminated against in the labour market as obesity rates have soared,[55] so there might not be any change if obesity rates start to fall. Or they might face even greater discrimination as their socially judged 'sinful' behaviour stands out more.

Back to drug laws. Assuming that the current laws need more scrutiny, one way to deal with the emotional reactions to drugs and drug users that contribute towards beliefism is to try and change those reactions. This could involve trying to take the heat out of the debate. We have already seen ways in which this might be done, most notably by taking a break at the start of any discussion or whenever you feel yourself or someone else getting emotionally overheated. It will be difficult to remind yourself or them to take a break in the heat of the debate, so this needs to be agreed to by all parties before debate takes place. It might involve the use of something akin to a time-out card that each party could use for themselves and/or to force the other side to take a break.

Changing the emotional reaction could also involve putting some different emotions in rather than taking all emotion out. We have also seen how positive moods can help open people's minds to different arguments, and so doing something 'happy making' before a discussion might help to make the discussion run more smoothly.[56] Another effective strategy could be playing upbeat music. In a classroom setting, teachers might begin with a fun and engaging warm-up activity to get students excited and ready to learn. In a business environment, managers could recognise and celebrate small wins before diving into more serious topics, thereby enhancing motivation and openness. Encouraging physical exercise is another option, since it has been shown to not only enhance mood but also to improve performance – and, in all likelihood, reduce beliefism.[57]

The discussion of drug laws is unlikely to be something that comes up in most workplaces, and this is probably a good thing given how divisive the issue appears to be (recall the 'avoidance' results at the start of the book). There is no problem at all with some subjects explicitly being off-limits in some environments. The political workplace is one environment within which there should be more discussion of drugs laws rather than less, though. Politicians could be encouraged to engage in mindfulness or deep-breathing exercises before any debate, and generally to practise stress reduction and mood enhancement. Those presenting the evidence should be given licence to step away from the debate if it becomes too heated. None of us are compelled to engage with someone who is being hostile, not even in hierarchical workplaces.

An alternative approach to changing emotional reactions is to accept them. Approaching an issue or a debate in a passionate way might drive us to drill down deeper into the evidence. But this can happen only if both ducks and rabbits are represented, and only if both sides are willing to calm down enough at some point to accept that the other side may have a point. These are the foundations upon which adversarial collaboration is built. In many ways, the select committees in the UK Parliament are built on the basis of bringing together politicians from all parties to consider issues relating to specific areas, such as health and social care, and work and pensions. To some extent, party allegiance makes clear each politician's prior beliefs but the discussion of drug laws, which cut across party lines, might require more transparency in people's starting positions. This approach will only work if we do more to celebrate those whose emotional minds are changed by robust evidence. I'm not especially optimistic about this, though, so perhaps it is best overall to try and take the emotion out before discussion begins.

The right to life

One of the most contentious issues over the past few decades, especially in the US, has been the abortion debate.[58] Religion and politics are much more entwined in the US than in the UK. I recall Alastair Campbell, one of the then UK prime minister Tony Blair's senior advisors, interrupting him twenty-plus years ago with the words 'We don't do God' when Blair was about to talk about his faith.[59] This is a good illustration of where some topics might legitimately be excluded from discussion in some contexts. Whenever the UK Parliament has voted on abortion it has been a 'free' vote, meaning that the MPs vote based on their personal preferences and not according to their political party's wishes.

From one extreme perspective, the right to life of an unborn child is seen to trump any consideration of a woman's right to choose. Human life begins at conception. I'll refer to this as the perspective of the 'foetal ducks'. Terminating a pregnancy is therefore morally equivalent to taking a life. Abortion is murder. Many religious teachings uphold the sanctity of life, though they rarely refer to abortion itself. For many this viewpoint is non-negotiable, with little room for exceptions, although in extreme cases involving rape and incest, and especially when the mother's life is at risk, many religious leaders consider abortion to be a legitimate course of action. The Roman Catholic Church, for example, acknowledges that medical treatments to save the life of the mother that indirectly result in the loss of the foetus are morally permissible. Orthodox Jewish law, or *halacha*, permits abortion if the mother's life is in danger. The principle of *pikuach nefesh* ('saving a life') takes precedence, and, where only one life can be saved, the mother's life is prioritised over the foetus.

From the other extreme perspective, women's rights and bodily autonomy trump the rights of an unborn child. This perspective emphasises personal freedom, choice, and the importance of safeguarding women's reproductive rights. Let's refer to this as the view of the 'maternal rabbits'. A pregnant woman has the right to terminate all the way up to the time of birth because the right to choose dominates the right to life. I'm going to come clean and say that this is my own view. A mother's right to self-determination holds for all the time she carries an unborn child. To my mind, a foetus has no right to life, a newborn baby does. The right to life starts at birth. How do my views on this issue make you feel? You don't have to feel anything, of course (about my views or me).

If the mother's life is going to turn out considerably less well if the baby lived, for example by having to bring up a severely disabled child, then there is a utilitarian argument for allowing for the termination of newborn babies. Allowing for infanticide, albeit in very limited circumstances, has been the view of the philosopher Peter Singer, perhaps the world's foremost utilitarian thinker. He argues that society should seek to maximise the welfare of sentient beings, i.e., animals that can perceive and feel things. Clearly, a mother is sentient whereas a newborn lacks the same moral status as they are not yet capable of forming intentions or understanding their existence. Singer's arguments have had a huge influence on animal rights campaigners.[60] He makes a coherent and compelling case for treating the killing of many of the animals we eat as tantamount to murder on the grounds of their sentience. I'm suspecting that you will have a lot more sympathy with his views about animal welfare than infanticide, which I suspect you may recoil at.

In the US, where religion is at the heart of the abortion debate, the overall percentage of people agreeing with abortion seems to be increasing over the past decades, mainly driven by a change in attitudes from the liberal side of the spectrum. From around 1980 to 2020, Democrats have shown an increasing trajectory of support, with a particularly steep rise after 2010, indicating strong and growing favourability towards abortion rights. Republicans, on the other hand, have consistently shown the lowest support for the statement, with very little change over the years and, if anything, a slight decline in recent years. Opinions can change, and polarise, in response to policy. Following the overturning of *Roe v. Wade* in 2021, which was a federal law providing women with the right to an abortion, data show that the proportion of Democrats supporting the statement that abortion should be legal in all or most cases goes from 79 per cent in 2020 to 85 per cent in 2022.[61]

In the UK, there has been a gradual increase in the acceptance of abortion over the past few decades. Public opinion now shows a majority pro-choice stance across the political spectrum. A survey conducted by Censuswide for the British Pregnancy Advisory Service (BPAS) revealed that 71 per cent of Brits agree that 'if a woman does not want to continue a pregnancy, she should be able to have an abortion'. This view is consistent across political affiliations, with 70 per cent of Conservative voters and 77 per cent of Labour voters in favour of abortion rights.[62] Currently, a woman who terminates a pregnancy outside of what is permitted by law can face criminal prosecution. This is very rare but there have recently been a couple of high-profile cases. In all likelihood, the UK Parliament will have fully decriminalised abortion by the time this book is published.

A 2012 YouGov poll showed that the public largely agrees with the current twenty-four-week limit for abortion, with half of the respondents considering it appropriate, though a quarter think it should be earlier, particularly older women.[63] There is strong support for abortion before twenty-four weeks under various conditions, such as risk to the mother's health or if the pregnancy is a result of rape. After twenty-four weeks, the support is more varied, but the majority still supports abortion when the mother's life is at risk or if there is a significant risk to the mother's health. As medical technology advances, we gain a clearer understanding of when a foetus can feel pain, when it can survive outside the womb, and the health implications for the prospective mother of late-term abortions. As we can save more babies born earlier in the gestation cycle, laws have sometimes changed to bring forward the legal limit for abortion e.g., from twenty-eight to twenty-four weeks.

I find the logic behind these changes unconvincing. It is not entirely clear to me why advances in science should be used to determine the ethics of the trade-off between the rights of a foetus and the rights to self-determination of a mother. And besides, evidence isn't just medical. Socio-economic and psychological studies highlight the implications of unwanted pregnancies on women's economic status, mental health and societal roles. Studies on the mental health implications of abortion for women indicate that the primary emotion is one of relief, but it is also common for many to feel grief, especially where the social norms are against abortion.[64] Moreover, there are always unintended consequences of any policy response. Evidence shows that restricting access to safe abortions doesn't necessarily reduce the number of abortions, but it can increase the number of unsafe procedures, leading to higher maternal mortality rates.[65]

So, all in all, it seems to me that the most sensical position on abortion is to grant a woman a right to bodily autonomy and a newborn a right to life. This is about as much of a maternal rabbit perspective as you would find today. As throughout, I would quite like to justify this on utilitarian grounds. I think a different conclusion to Peter Singer is reached if the benefits of those who adopt an unwanted baby are accounted for. Evidence on the full flow of costs and benefits of different abortion policies would assist in settling the dispute but if I'm being perfectly honest, I don't think I will budge from my position on abortion because the evidence will never be compelling enough for me to do so. This highlights just how limiting evidence can be in changing people's minds. I might not change my mind, but I will nonetheless listen to those who disagree with me and especially to their views on other issues.

Embracing exposure to reduce beliefism in relation to abortion

A natural reaction from those who disagree with me or with ardent pro-lifers, say, is to respond by being very beliefist. This is a mistake. We should accept that some people will have extreme and immovable views and remind ourselves that this is a healthy characteristic of a well-functioning society. We must remind ourselves that someone who disagrees with us can still be kind, funny and have good ideas. I must admit that religion-driven pro-life views on abortion are probably the hardest context in which to remind myself of this. Restrictions on abortion cause such harms to women that I struggle to engage with those who are willing to tolerate those harms in the name of religion. But I would still like to discuss abortion with them if they would discuss it with me. And I definitely want to hear about their ideas for increasing productivity.

We have already seen how one of the most effective ways to reduce beliefism and its various spillovers is through the final E of EMBRACE – exposure to the out-group and their beliefs. This is difficult but important in the case of abortion. From our survey of the Fab 500, there was very little difference in the 'avoid ratings' of ducks or rabbits across the six issues discussed here. The exception was abortion, where those adopting the 'foetal duck' perspective were much more likely to want to avoid those who disagreed with them about abortion. These people need to be encouraged to expose themselves to 'maternal rabbits' – and the rabbits need to try to expose themselves to the ducks. Reducing beliefism is a two-way street. One, relatively less beliefist, group might have to reach out first for the harmful effects of beliefism spillovers to be reduced.

For Allport's contact hypothesis to be successful, recall from earlier that four conditions must be met: 1) the groups should have shared goals; 2) there should be the potential for cross-group friendships; 3) the groups should perceive each other as having equal status; and 4) there should be broad institutional support for interaction.[66] On the face of it, the first condition in the context of abortion is the most challenging. The goal of pro-lifers is the welfare of the foetus and the goal of the pro-choicers is the welfare of the mother. This makes any compromise over beliefs very difficult – but our aim is to influence beliefism and not beliefs. If the shared goal is a willingness to see past different beliefs on abortion properly to engage with the person or group and their beliefs on other issues, then we have a more tractable problem.

Witnessing first-hand the kindness, humour and good ideas of a pro-lifer when you're pro-choice and vice versa is one of the most powerful ways to reduce beliefism and its spillovers. During the course of writing this book, I have sought to expose myself to people of different faiths, who are more inclined to be against abortion and to have views on other issues, such as gay marriage, with which I disagree strongly. I often strike up conversations on public transport and in public places, and I have used these as opportunities to get into discussions of God as often and as quickly as the person and situation allows. The good thing about this environment is that friendships could be formed (the second condition of contact theory) and the conversations are between people of equal status (as required by the third condition of contact theory). Perhaps you can think of ways of exposing yourself a bit more . . . stop it, you know what I mean . . .

Not one of my 'train friends' has changed my mind that a woman should have the right to terminate a pregnancy right up to the point of birth. Most of them have been thoroughly decent people. By dint of being in contact with them, I have become more tolerant towards people of faith. I went for a few beers a few weeks ago with a couple of guys I met on the train from London to Brighton, one of whom turned out to be religious and against abortion. Experiences like this serve to remind me/us that we are so much more than our beliefs and that we have very little choice over what we believe in any case. At the same time, I would not want the religious man's views on abortion and other matters that are directly related to his faith to have much impact on public policy. While I might have few red lines when it comes to personal relationships, I have more when it comes to environments where someone else's beliefs might harm other people. 'We don't do God' in policymaking in the UK, and I think we are better off for it.

As with drugs, the workplace probably isn't the place for discussions of abortion. This is not to say that discussion of it should be suppressed, just that there would need to be a point relevant to the company for it to be raised. Politicians need to discuss it more often, of course, and they should spend more time with people who disagree with them about abortion and in general. Some people are appalled when they see politicians of different parties socialising or joking together. I'm not. Quite the contrary; I think it shows a healthy willingness not to split on someone. And it leads to better policy as the harms from beliefism spillovers are mitigated through interaction and exposure. Parliament and the government can signal their support for interaction by practising what they preach and providing incentives for a duck and a rabbit to walk into a bar. MPs in the UK generally don't need much incentive to go to the bar, so this should be a relatively easy ask.

18

Predictably inconsistent

Duck in the rabbit?

Having gone through several issues at breakneck speed, it would be easier on your brain, and in how you decide to treat me in a beliefist world, if you could predict my views on issue Z from knowing them on issues X and Y. Having established my 'lefty-duck' credentials in relation to economic inequality, if I was younger, I would then perhaps be more likely to be a duck in relation to immigration (open-door duck) and climate change (mitigating duck). But, as an old git, I am, in fact, a rabbit in both cases, even if only mildly so (restricting and adapting).[67] My views on rights are very libertarian. On freedom of speech, I am a permitting duck rather than a censorious rabbit. On self-determination, I am a very libertarian duck rather than a paternalistic rabbit. These views are predictable from one another but less so from my views about economic inequality. On abortion, I am a maternal rabbit rather than a foetal duck. In the UK, the most important predictor of views about abortion is religion (and I'm not religious).

Overall, I come out on various political preference surveys as a left libertarian. I think that probably makes my natural home the Liberal Democrats in the UK. If only Britain had a more proportional electoral system, eh? Once upon a time, I would have defined myself as 'progressive' but that is now a term which has been appropriated by, or at least can be apportioned to, those who can sometimes be quite beliefist.[68] A lack of tolerance is one value, perhaps, that unites far left and far right.[69] During my twenties and thirties, I cared much more about the 'left part' of me. I feel just as strongly about the 'libertarian part' of me these days. The assumptions that were made about the strength of my views on Brexit and the madness of the consensus about the policy responses to Covid have played a big part in this shift. I think the left of British politics has also lost sight of some of its 'bread and butter' issues relating to inequalities by social class.

Interesting patterns are evident in our survey of the Fab 500 when we look for ducks or rabbits based on people's responses to the three pairs of questions for each of fairness and rights. The tables overleaf show the number of people who fall into the eight groups based on their responses to the two sets of questions. It is worth saying at this point that the table is based on only about half the sample because the other half answered the question pairs in ways that make it hard for us to say whether they are a duck or a rabbit on that issue. This shows, once more, that people can be quite odd. Or more precisely, that many beliefs are constructed and do not sit deeply within our minds. As noted before, the ephemeral nature of our beliefs and the way they can be so influenced by framing effects makes the extent of beliefism in society all the more remarkable.

Insofar as we can say anything meaningful from the responses of the Fab 500, there is very little relationship between the responses to the fairness questions and to the rights-based ones. This is interesting because these data suggest that we should be careful about making assumptions in relation to someone's beliefs on freedom of speech, say, even if we already knew their views about inequality, immigration and climate change. I am heartened by the lack of predictability. When it comes to fairness on its own, 31 per cent are duck throughout and 25 per cent are rabbit throughout, i.e., over half of the sample could be described as having beliefs that are in some senses 'predictable'. My own beliefs on fairness – duck, rabbit, rabbit (DRR) – are shared by 7 per cent of the sample. In relation to rights, we might expect views on freedom of speech to be associated with views on self-determination but only 43 per cent are either duck *or* rabbit on both these questions. My own beliefs on rights – rabbit, rabbit, rabbit (RRR) – are shared by 10 per cent of the sample. Overall, across all questions, only 2 per cent of the sample think like me . . . oh well.

	Fairness	Rights
DDD	31%	14%
DRD	9%	17%
DDR	5%	10%
DRR	7%	14%
RDR	12%	12%
RDD	7%	12%
RRD	5%	9%
RRR	25%	10%

Recent and much more robust work in the US suggests that conservatives might be more inclined towards deontological

ethics, valuing tradition, authority and absolute moral principles, while liberals might lean towards teleological ethics,
emphasising outcomes and the welfare of the broader community.[70] These tendencies are not absolute and can vary
widely among individuals within each political group. A 2021
meta-analysis looked at the connection between morality and
political orientation.[71] By conducting an extensive literature
review across major databases, the researchers gathered data
from 33,804 participants across eighty-nine studies, plus
192,870 participants from the YourMorals.org website. The
study confirms the fundamental differences in moral foundations between conservatives and liberals but also suggests
that it's hard to make sweeping statements about either group.

Having said that, the Pew Research Center has found that
ideological consistency, which refers to the extent to which
individuals in the US hold uniformly liberal or conservative
views across a range of issues, has grown over time.[72] This
growth is more pronounced among those with postgraduate
and college education. The rise in ideological consistency
also varies by age and education. Millennials tend to be more
liberal than older generations while younger Republicans are
not so different to older Republicans. More highly educated
people are more likely to express consistently liberal views
while those with less education are much less likely to hold
ideologically consistent views.[73] This evidence points to a
general pattern in the literature on issue polarisation; namely,
that 'radical progressives' have quickly become the most iden-
tifiable and predictable group in society.[74]

It is unclear which underlying values matter most to people
when they're judging or discriminating against other people.
Research on affective polarisation and beliefism that directly
compare differences in economic values versus cultural ones,
for example, is largely absent. But recent data indicate that,

when it comes to the drivers of affective polarisation, economic grievances and views about the government's tax and spend policies are often overshadowed by battles over cultural values.[75] This suggests that differences in views and behaviours relating to drug use, for example, can be more salient than differences in views about redistribution in shaping divisions in society. Moreover, those with authoritarian tendencies are more likely to exhibit greater intolerance towards different identities and observable behaviours than towards economic differences among people.[76]

I have stressed at various points how important transparency is in our attempts to reduce beliefism and its spillovers. So, I have sought to be as transparent as possible in articulating my own beliefs in Part 3 of the book. I went around many versions of the text here before settling on this one, and I'm still not entirely happy with it. The issues are complicated, the evidence is constantly evolving, and my mind is far from made up about some of the issues. As I said, I'm 'exposing' myself in large part so that you can reflect on your reactions towards the values I've articulated in this part of book. I hope you think I'm a reasonable person even if you think I'm wrong about some things. In the very least, I hope you wouldn't want completely to avoid me. How much of your reaction to me do you think stems from a gut instinct about how the issues ought to be approached? Or from a perception of a deeper understanding of the issues than me? Or from something else?

A fair and free innings?

I know this is not a book about beliefs, but – not least because only 2 per cent of the Fab 500 share my views – I'm going to briefly outline my overarching framework for approaching any issue. I made the case in Part 1 that the legitimacy of our beliefs about how the world ought to be are dependent on our willingness to live by the costs and benefits of their enactment. So, I'll briefly describe how I approach those costs and benefits. I think that *safety-net libertarianism* would be the best way to describe my approach. The basic idea is for the state to intervene to protect and support the worst off in society and when people fall on tough times (the safety-net part) while at the same time getting the fuck out of everyone else's lives (the libertarian bit). I'm not the first to come up with such an idea, and everything is in the detail.[77]

Let me elaborate on how I would operationalise safety-net libertarianism, which may further flush out the basis upon which you might agree or disagree with me. It is my firmly held view that we should use the lifetime as the unit of analysis for assessing suffering and related inequalities. In other words, to look at the area under the lifetime happiness (or misery) curves of different individuals and groups. We can't say how deserving of support from the safety net someone is by simply taking a snapshot moment of their life. Rather, we need to estimate how good their life will be overall, from birth to death. All else equal, a longer life is better than a shorter one and a happier life is better than a less happy one. A longer, less happy life may or may not be better than a shorter, happier life depending on the relative differences in life expectancy and happiness. But the point here, all else equal, is that the lower the area under someone's lifetime happiness curve, the more deserving of support they are from the safety net.

This would mean giving greater priority to the lives of younger over older people. At the beginning of my academic career, Alan Williams convinced me that those with the lowest prospects for wellbeing over their lifetime should have the greatest claim on resources. This is the essence of the *fair innings argument* (FIA).[78] The shorter and worse your life is, the greater the priority you should be afforded. I become increasingly convinced of the merits of the FIA as I get older (as I would increasingly be disadvantaged by its application). It's the lifetime wot matters. Danny Kahneman was in favour of the FIA, and we spoke about it a lot during the pandemic. He advised me that I shouldn't make too much of it at the time simply because the climate of fear was such that policymakers would ignore me. He was right, as he was about so much.

The Covid pandemic really was the time to have a grown-up conversation about death and dying, but we blew it. We got caught up in an existential crisis where every death, irrespective of age and frailty, was seen as a tragedy. The average life expectancy for an eighteen-year-old in the UK today is around eighty-one. According to the Office for National Statistics, around 60 per cent of the deaths from Covid-19 in the UK were people of this age or older. Substantively, most of those who were asked to bear the biggest burden from social distancing measures, school closures, etc. (some of which directly impact negatively on life expectancy), won't live for as long as those who died from Covid. This is unfair. You don't have to be old – like Alan or Danny or, increasingly, me – to agree. You just need to step back from a given moment in time to look at the lifetime – to consider not only what is to come but also what has come before.

I understand completely if you're feeling a little uneasy about discriminating against older people. A lot has to do with the framing, of course, and you ought to react a little more favourably to the notion of prioritising younger people. Beyond semantics, there is a substantive difference between discriminating by age as compared to doing so by race, gender, etc. Every older person was once young, so the discrimination can be seen as being akin to different priority weights for the same person at different points in time. Discrimination by other characteristics is more clearly across different people at the same point in time. I was twenty-five and hope to see seventy-five (with associated priority weights attached) but I'm never going to be black. I should say that there are plenty of preference and survey data out there showing that the public broadly agree with me that there is a difference between discriminating by age compared to other factors such as race, gender and sexuality. The FIA is therefore a conceptually robust and empirically reliable conception of justice.[79]

The area under the lifetime happiness curve serves as a founding stone alongside which my other core belief, libertarianism, can be placed. It's not for the government to foist longer lives on us in ways that they would prefer but which we may not. We should all be allowed to make trade-offs between length and quality of life. It's for the state to provide the conditions under which we can be happy in ways consistent with our preferences and given the circumstances we face. I appreciate that seeking to reduce inequalities over the lifetime and preserving liberty will sometimes come into conflict with one another. I'm sure you'll be able to point out several inconsistencies to me. But I don't claim to have all the answers and no single overarching framework is going to be suitable in all contexts. I'm trying to be as transparent as I can here, and I am happy for contextual factors to impact upon how I resolve the tensions between my concerns for lifetime happiness on the one hand and libertarianism on the other.

Here's an example to illustrate the tension. I have long (but not always) wondered why some people say they wouldn't give money to a homeless person if they knew that they would spend it on booze. Why not? Why not trust that person's ability to choose what they spend their money on given their preferences and circumstances? If you consider that a homeless person is more prone to bad decisions, perhaps by virtue of being homeless, then give your money to a homeless charity or to causes seeking to reduce homelessness. If you're going to give money to the homeless person directly, the least you can do is to afford them the same respect as you do your colleagues at work when you buy them a round of drinks. The kind of safety-net libertarianism I have in mind would make reducing homelessness a high priority because life on the streets is hard and mostly miserable. But *given* that someone is homeless, I wouldn't doubly punish them by not respecting their preferences *given* their circumstances.

Regardless of how you feel about my beliefs, the important point here as throughout is that being alert to the costs and benefits of a belief is a necessary condition for us to have some intellectual skin in the game – and in being willing to listen to someone who disagrees with us. We can quite reasonably downplay someone's beliefs when they refuse to acknowledge trade-offs. Given that we typically witness better outcomes with more transparency than with less, we should seek to flush out the trade-offs that we believe are being made and those that we think should be made between different attributes of value in as many decision contexts as is feasible. By accepting that safety-net libertarianism is not without its downsides and inconsistencies, I hope that I am going some way towards not only flushing out the issues but also providing an environment conducive to less beliefism.

19

EMBRACE the duck–rabbit problem

Although the strength of my duck or rabbit preference differs across the six issues discussed here, I care deeply about all six issues *per se*, and I also care deeply about your right to disagree with me. Just as we can take someone's kindness as a sign of weakness, it is possible to take someone's willingness to engage in debate as a sign of a weakness of opinion. Kindness and a willingness to engage with someone else's beliefs are, in fact, both signs of strength. There are (nearly) always at least two sides to an argument. Could you be friends with someone who disagrees on all (or most of) these issues, or share a pint while navigating your way through these contentious discussions? Would you have a beer with me? How can each of us, and the organisations and institutions we work for and interact with, be less beliefist and more open-minded towards those who see a rabbit when we see a duck? How can we limit the harms caused by beliefism? These questions probe the depth of our commitment to reducing beliefism.

I know that you're now committed to reducing beliefism and its various spillover effects. You wouldn't have got this far if you weren't. Thank you for your commitment to less beliefism and for reading this book (or else jumping straight to the end, I suppose). I wonder whether you're less beliefist as a result. Shall we find out? Let's go back to the beginning. Here's half-a-dozen of the 'avoid questions' that were at the start of the book, and which relate to the issues we've just discussed. Please rate how much you would want to avoid someone based on them having polar opposite views to you. I guess I hope that you would want to avoid them less now, but if you don't then at least your journey through this book has confirmed that you're right to avoid those nasty people who disagree with you. If you've become more avoiding, then, well, I really don't know what to say.

	Not avoid at all					Completely avoid				
Economic equality	0	1	2	3	4	5	6	7	8	9	10
Immigration	0	1	2	3	4	5	6	7	8	9	10
Environmental issues	0	1	2	3	4	5	6	7	8	9	10
Freedom of Speech	0	1	2	3	4	5	6	7	8	9	10
Illicit drug use	0	1	2	3	4	5	6	7	8	9	10
Abortion	0	1	2	3	4	5	6	7	8	9	10

Regardless, we know that we can't simply 'will ourselves' less beliefist. We must instead embed it into our interactions and create a 'meta-environment' to make using EMBRACE the norm rather than the exception. I trust that you are now a little more committed than before to a world where different perspectives and people are listened to. It won't be easy, but it can perhaps be made slightly more manageable by accepting that each of us is full of contradictions and a fair dose of hypocrisy.[80] By acknowledging these facts of the human condition, we can approach our interactions with more humility and less judgement. While we're all motivated to be happier, say, we're not all motivated to be less beliefist. It does become a much more tractable challenge, though, if we are willing to accept that, in many ways, beliefism is our default position that we cannot simply think ourselves out of.

Powered by EMBRACE, we can do more to seek out different viewpoints that challenge our cognitive biases and strengthen our ability to adapt and evolve. In so doing, we can become a little more accepting of ambiguity, which is vital in a world where so much is uncertain and unpredictable. Wherever the image of the duck is dominant, it will most often be good for individuals and society if the rabbit could be seen – and heard – a little more, and vice versa. At the same time as enabling more people to feel comfortable in airing their views, a less beliefist world would also encourage those without strong views on a particular topic to say that they haven't yet made up their minds, or that they don't know enough about the subject, or that they simply don't care enough about it. Less beliefism includes accepting different strengths as well as kinds of beliefs.

As we wrap up our exploration of beliefism, we should all reflect on the practical steps that we can take to incorporate the EMBRACE framework more deeply into our everyday lives and institutional practices in ways that will enrich people's lives, improve the bottom line, and advance social progress. It is for all of us – private citizens and parents, practitioners and policymakers, employees and employers – actively to design our interactions and organisational structures to be less beliefist. It is through deliberate design and committed action that we can transform the EMBRACE principles from abstract ideas into everyday practices. This is my call to arms.

Less beliefism won't be easy and the journey might not always be pleasurable – but progress depends on it, and it feels purposeful. One of the main takeaways for me from writing this book is that I'm going to listen more to different beliefs – and I'm going to do that in ways that contain a considerable degree of humour and play. The challenges we face are serious ones, but they will be better addressed when we don't take ourselves too seriously. I look forward to discussing with you how best to embrace different perspectives and people – and to disagreeing along the way. Let's do it over a drink (a non-alcoholic one if you prefer). A duck and a rabbit walk into a bar . . .

Acknowledgements

I enjoy writing this bit, but it does make me feel a bit nervous about forgetting someone. So many people contribute towards making a book a better version of itself and I apologise if you've been left off here. Let me start with the one person it would be impossible to forget – George Melios. You have provided the very highest quality research assistance throughout. In drawing my attention to so many books and articles you helped to shape the conceptualisation and direction of *Beliefism*. But way beyond all this, you were always there for a chat, not just as a colleague but as a friend. Thank you, George.

Two other people who have been there from the beginning are my agent Will Francis and my editor Holly Harley. Thank you both so much for supporting me at all stages of development, for providing super helpful comments on drafts and, perhaps above all, for emboldening me to write exactly as I would like to. Big thanks also to Amanda Henwood and Aleks Matic for taking the time to provide detailed comments on a final draft. I trust you can see how much better the final version is as a result. Thanks to Howard Watson for providing final edits.

I would like to thank my wife, Les, and kids, Poppy and Stanley, for doing so much more than simply bearing with me during this process. This is the third book you've gone through with me, and you all continue to inspire, shape and inform my writing — sometimes through shouting, always with humour. Thanks also to my best mate in Brighton, Jason, who has had to put up with me discussing the book with him, and for making sure I have a tea, coffee or beer in my hand when we do.

I am so grateful to all the academic colleagues and friends who, through various conversations, have helped to shape my thinking and provide useful references along the way. Those that come most to mind as I write this are: Sonja Belkin, David Bradford, Priya Halai, Richard Layard, Laura Kudrna, Kate Laffan, Robert Metcalfe, Olivier Sibony, Yara Sleiman and Rim Turkmani. Thanks to the EMSc Behavioural Science students at LSE who engaged with my early ideas around the EMBRACE framework.

I would like to thank all those at Boston and Harvard who found the time to talk to me about *Beliefism* when I visited in 2024: Taylor Boas, Jacob Brown, Melani Cammett, Ryan Enos, Joshua Greene, Carey Morewedge, Vincent Pons and Tali Sharot. A special thanks to Dan Gilbert and Cass Sunstein. And while thinking about the US, I would like to dedicate a thank you to Danny Kahneman, who died in March 2024 and who was an inspiration and a friend for the past twenty-plus years.

A big thanks to Steve Baker, Rob Henderson, James Marriot, Gus O'Donnell, Rory Sutherland and Matthew Syed for general conversations, as well as their writings, that have shaped the ways I think about beliefism and related issues. And they have influenced what I do about it, too. For example, Steve and I have created 'The Provocation People' to embed tolerance by design into organisations (see theprovocationpeople.com).

A final and huge thanks to Kirstie Hepburn for reading through the whole manuscript, for continuing to ensure that my professional life retains some kind of order, and for always being at the other end of the phone when I need to rant about something. I just need to get you to pronounce scone properly.

Notes

PART 1: TAKING SIDES

1   M. P. Winslow, A. Aaron and E. N. Amadife (2011), 'African Americans' lay theories about the detection of prejudice and nonprejudice', *Journal of Black Studies* 42(1): 43–70, www.jstor.org/stable/25780791.
2   D. F. Stone (2023), *Undue Hate: A Behavioral Economic Analysis of Hostile Polarization in US Politics and Beyond*, Cambridge, MA: MIT Press.
3   L. Diamond and L. Morlino (2004), 'The quality of democracy: An overview', *Journal of Democracy* 15(4): 20–31, https://doi.org/10.1353/jod.2004.0060.
4   M. Olson (2022), *The Rise and Decline of Nations*, New Haven: Yale University Press.
5   L. Wittgenstein (2001), *Philosophical Investigations*, translated by G. E. M. Anscombe, 3rd ed., Oxford: Blackwell.
6   M. Graso et al. (2022), 'The dark side of belief in COVID-19 scientists and scientific evidence', *Personality and Individual Differences*, 193: 111594.
7   D. O. Hebb (2005), *The Organization of Behavior: A Neuropsychological Theory*, London and New York: Psychology Press.
8   P. Brugger and S. Brugger (1993), 'The Easter bunny in October: Is it disguised as a duck?', *Perceptual and Motor Skills* 76(2): 577–8.
9   A. M. Lokhorst et al. (2013), 'Commitment and behavior change: A meta-analysis and critical review of commitment-making strategies in environmental research', *Environment and Behavior* 45(1): 3–34.

10   Z. Kunda (1990), 'The case for motivated reasoning', *Psychological Bulletin* 108(3): 480.

11   A. Williams (1997), 'Intergenerational equity: an exploration of the "fair innings" argument', *Health Economics* 6(2): 117–32.

12   L. Ross (1977), 'The intuitive psychologist and his shortcomings: Distortions in the attribution process', in Leonard Berkowitz (ed.), *Advances in Experimental Social Psychology*, New York: Academic Press, vol. 10, pp. 173–220.

13   Pew Research Center (October 2017), 'The partisan divide on political values grows even wider', www.pewresearch.org/politics/2017/10/05/the-partisan-divide-on-political-values-grows-even-wider/ (accessed 24 July 2024).

14   W. J. Chopik and M. Motyl (2016), 'Ideological fit enhances interpersonal orientations', *Social Psychological and Personality Science* 7(8): 759–68; E. Bakshy, S. Messing and L. A. Adamic (2015), 'Exposure to ideologically diverse news and opinion on Facebook', *Science* 348(6239): 1130–2.

15   B. Duffy et al. (2019), 'Divided Britain: Polarisation and fragmentation trends in the UK', https://api.semanticscholar.org/CorpusID:210304925.

16   Gallup (2024), 'Women become more liberal; men mostly stable', https://news.gallup.com/poll/609914/women-become-liberal-men-mostly-stable.aspx; John Burn-Murdoch (2024), 'A new global gender divide is emerging', *Financial Times*, 26 January, www.ft.com/content/29fd9b5c-2f35-41bf-9d4c-994db4e12998 (both accessed 15 May 2024).

17   Y. Sleiman, G. Melios and P. Dolan (2023), '"Sleeping with the Enemy": Partisan sorting in online dating', 1 August, https://ssrn.com/abstract=4589420 or http://dx.doi.org/10.2139/ssrn.4589420.

18   J. Surowiecki (2005), *The Wisdom of Crowds*, New York: Anchor.

19   P. Dolan and M. M. Galizzi (2015), 'Like ripples on a pond: Behavioral spillovers and their implications for research and policy', *Journal of Economic Psychology* 47: 1–16; D. Krpan, M. M. Galizzi and P. Dolan (2019), 'Looking at spillovers in the mirror: Making a case for "behavioral spillunders"', *Frontiers in Psychology* 10: 422667.

20   A. I. Abramowitz (2021), 'November. Peak polarization? The rise of partisan-ideological consistency and its consequences', prepared for delivery at the State of the Parties Conference, Ray Bliss Institute, University of Akron.

21   M. Dimock (2014), 'Political polarization in the American public: How increasing ideological uniformity and partisan antipathy affect politics, compromise and everyday life', Pew Research Center, www.pewresearch.org/politics/2014/06/12/political-polarization-in-the-american-public/ (accessed 13 August 2024).

22   B. Klein Teeselink and G. Melios (2022), 'Partisanship, Government Responsibility, and Charitable Donations', https://ssrn.com/abstract=4189400 or http://dx.doi.org/10.2139/ssrn.4189400.

23 P. J. Egan (2020), 'Identity as dependent variable: How Americans shift their identities to align with their politics', *American Journal of Political Science* 64(3): 699–716.

24 S. B. Hobolt, T. J. Leeper and J. Tilley (2021), 'Divided by the vote: Affective polarization in the wake of the Brexit referendum', *British Journal of Political Science* 51(4): 1476–93.

25 J. Marks et al. (2019), 'Epistemic spillovers: Learning others' political views reduces the ability to assess and use their expertise in nonpolitical domains', *Cognition* 188: 74–84.

26 K. Michelitch (2015), 'Does electoral competition exacerbate interethnic or interpartisan economic discrimination? Evidence from a field experiment in market price bargaining', *American Political Science Review* 109(1): 43–61.

27 C. McConnell et al. (2018), 'The economic consequences of partisanship in a polarized era', *American Journal of Political Science* 62(1): 5–18.

28 S. E. Asch (2016), 'Effects of group pressure upon the modification and distortion of judgments', in L. W. Porter, H. L. Angle and R. W. Allen (eds), *Organizational Influence Processes*, 2nd edition, London: Routledge, pp. 295–303; M. Hallsworth et al. (2017), 'The behavioralist as tax collector: Using natural field experiments to enhance tax compliance', *Journal of Public Economics* 148: 14–31.

29 M. McPherson, L. Smith-Lovin and J. M. Cook (2001), 'Birds of a feather: Homophily in social networks', *Annual Review of Sociology* 27(1): 415–44.

30 Y. Zhang and J. van Hook (2009), 'Marital dissolution among interracial couples', *Journal of Marriage and Family* 71(1): 95–107.

31 D. M. Wegner (1987), 'Transactive memory: A contemporary analysis of the group mind', in B. Mullen and G. R. Goethals (eds), *Theories of Group Behavior*, New York: Springer, pp. 185–208.

32 I. L. Janis (2008), 'Groupthink', *IEEE Engineering Management Review* 36(1): 36.

33 I. L. Janis (1982), *Groupthink: Psychological Studies of Policy Decisions and Fiascos*, Boston: Houghton Mifflin.

34 S. E. Asch (1956), 'Studies of independence and conformity: I. A minority of one against a unanimous majority', *Psychological Monographs: General and Applied* 70(9): 1.

35 T. Kuran and C. R. Sunstein (1998), 'Availability cascades and risk regulation', *Stanford Law Review* 51: 683.

36 J. Kay (1996), *The Business of Economics*, Oxford: Oxford University Press.

37 J. K. Galbraith (1977), *A Life in Our Times: Memoirs*, Boston: Houghton Mifflin.

38 M. Scheffer et al. (2022), 'Belief traps: Tackling the inertia of harmful beliefs', *Proceedings of the National Academy of Sciences* 119(32): e2203149119.

39   C. Doherty et al. (2022), 'As partisan hostility grows, signs of frustration with the two-party system', Pew US Politics & Policy, 9 August, pp. 1–78, www.pewresearch.org/politics/2022/08/09/as-partisan-hostility-grows-signs-of-frustration-with-the-two-party-system/.

40   L. Boxell, M. Gentzkow and J. M. Shapiro (2024), 'Cross-country trends in affective polarization', *Review of Economics and Statistics* 106(2): 557–65.

41   I. H. Indridason (2011), 'Coalition formation and polarisation', *European Journal of Political Research* 50(5): 689–718.

42   J. Phillips (2022), 'Affective polarization: Over time, through the generations, and during the lifespan', *Political Behavior* 44: 1483–1508, https://doi.org/10.1007/s11109-022-09784-4.

43   K. Lawall et al. (2024), 'Negative political identities and costly political action', *Journal of Politics*, forthcoming.

44   W. D. Bradford and P. Dolan (2010), 'Getting used to it: The adaptive global utility model', *Journal of Health Economics* 29(6): 811–20.

45   E. Harteveld and M. Wagner (2023), 'Does affective polarisation increase turnout? Evidence from Germany, The Netherlands and Spain', *West European Politics* 46(4): 732–59.

46   T. R. Mitchell et al. (1997), 'Temporal adjustments in the evaluation of events: The "rosy view"', *Journal of Experimental Social Psychology* 33(4): 421–48.

47   D. Howell (1987), 'Goodbye to all that?: A review of literature on the 1984/5 miners' strike', *Work, Employment and Society* 1(3): 388–404.

48   G. Melios, T. Walsh and P. Dolan (2023), 'Aborting the confirmation bias? News consumption following the overturn of Roe v. Wade', 10 September, available at SSRN: https://papers.ssrn.com/sol3/papers.cfm?abstract_id=4944496.

49   A. F. Thimsen (2022), 'What is performative activism?', *Philosophy & Rhetoric* 55(1): 83–9.

50   K. Garimella et al. (2018), 'Political discourse on social media: Echo chambers, gatekeepers, and the price of bipartisanship', published at The Web Conference 2018, pp. 913–22, https://arxiv.org/abs/1801.01665.

51   H. Tian and H. Yerbury (2022), '"I'm in the center of a vortex": Mapping the affective experiences of trolling victims'. *First Monday* 27(10), 3 October 2022.

52   K. Laffan, C. Sunstein and P. Dolan (2024), 'Facing it: Assessing the immediate emotional impacts of calorie labelling using automatic facial coding', *Behavioural Public Policy* 8(3): 572–89.

53   S. Feldman (1988), 'Structure and consistency in public opinion: The role of core beliefs and values', *American Journal of Political Science* 32(2): 416–40.

54   J. Elster (2016), *Sour Grapes*, Cambridge: Cambridge University Press.

55   A. K. Sen (1977), 'Rational fools: A critique of the behavioral foundations of economic theory', *Philosophy & Public Affairs* 6(4): 317–44.

56   M. Yanovskiy and Y. Socol (2022), 'Are lockdowns effective in

managing pandemics?', *International Journal of Environmental Research and Public Health* 19(15): 9295.

57 Global Disinformation Index, homepage, www.disinformationindex.org (accessed 16 May 2024).

58 J. Farrell and M. Rabin (1996), 'Cheap talk', *Journal of Economic Perspectives* 10(3): 103–18.

59 N. N. Taleb (2018), *Skin in the Game: Hidden Asymmetries in Daily Life*, New York: Random House.

60 S. Pinker (2003), *The Blank Slate: The Modern Denial of Human Nature*, London: Penguin.

61 A. Bandura and R. H. Walters (1977), *Social Learning Theory*, vol. 1, Englewood Cliffs: Prentice Hall.

62 R. B. Zajonc (1968), 'Attitudinal effects of mere exposure', *Journal of Personality and Social Psychology* 9(2, pt 2): 1.

63 J. Haidt (2012), *The Righteous Mind: Why Good People Are Divided by Politics and Religion*, New York: Vintage.

64 R. Plomin (2019), *Blueprint: How DNA Makes Us Who We Are*, Cambridge, MA: MIT Press.

65 S. M. Myers (1996), 'An interactive model of religiosity inheritance: The importance of family context', *American Sociological Review* 61(5): 858–66.

66 M. J. Meaney (2001), 'Maternal care, gene expression, and the transmission of individual differences in stress reactivity across generations', *Annual Review of Neuroscience* 24(1): 1161–92.

67 J. L. Heckman (2008), 'Schools, skills, and synapses', *Economic Inquiry* 46(3): 289–324.

68 T. J. Leeper and R. Slothuus (2014), 'Political parties, motivated reasoning, and public opinion formation', *Political Psychology* 35: 129–56.

69 J. Lorenzo-Rodríguez and M. Torcal (2023), 'Twitter and affective polarisation: following political leaders in Spain', in M. Torcal (ed.), *Affective Polarisation in Spain*, London: Routledge, pp. 95–121.

70 R. D. Enos (2017), *The Space Between Us: Social Geography and Politics*, Cambridge: Cambridge University Press.

71 E. Cantoni and V. Pons (2022), 'Does context outweigh individual characteristics in driving voting behavior? Evidence from relocations within the United States', *American Economic Review* 112(4): 1226–72.

72 J. R. Brown et al. (2023), 'The effect of childhood environment on political behavior: Evidence from young US movers, 1992–2021', National Bureau of Economic Research Working Paper No. w31759, https://papers.ssrn.com/sol3/papers.cfm?abstract_id=4596059.

73 S. Stephens-Davidowitz (2018), 'The songs that bind', *New York Times*, 10 February, www.nytimes.com/2018/02/10/opinion/sunday/favorite-songs.html (accessed 13 August 2024).

74 P. Dolan (2020), *Happy Ever After: A Radical New Approach to Living Well*, London: Penguin.

75 Morgan Smith (2023), 'This is the happiest job in the world, according to new research: "You get to see the fruits of your labor"', CNBC, 29 September, www.cnbc.com/2023/09/29/this-is-the-happiest-job-in-the-world-according-to-new-research.html (accessed 13 August 2024).

76 A. Whiting et al. (2019), 'The importance of selecting the right messenger: A framed field experiment on recycled water products', *Ecological Economics* 161: 1–8.

77 BBC News (2020), 'Marcus Rashford brings food brand giants together to tackle child food poverty', 1 September, www.bbc.com/news/uk-53979648 (accessed 12 August 2024).

78 D. Gray, H. Pickard and L. Munford (2021), 'Election outcomes and individual subjective wellbeing in Great Britain', *Economica* 88(351): 809–37.

79 S. Pinto et al. (2021), 'Presidential elections, divided politics, and happiness in the USA', *Economica* 88(349): 189–207.

80 M. S. Kimball et al. (2024), 'Happiness Dynamics, Reference Dependence, and Motivated Beliefs in US Presidential Elections', National Bureau of Economic Research Working Paper No. w32078.

81 B. Radcliff (2001), 'Politics, markets, and life satisfaction: The political economy of human happiness', *American Political Science Review* 95(4): 939–52.

82 G. Ward et al. (2021), '(Un) happiness and voting in US presidential elections', *Journal of Personality and Social Psychology* 120(2): 370.

83 A. Bor and M. B. Petersen (2022), 'The psychology of online political hostility: A comprehensive, cross-national test of the mismatch hypothesis', *American Political Science Review* 116(1): 1–18.

84 S. S. Nayak et al. (2021), 'Is divisive politics making Americans sick? Associations of perceived partisan polarization with physical and mental health outcomes among adults in the United States', *Social Science & Medicine* 284: 113976.

85 M. F. Scheier, C. S. Carver and M. W. Bridges (2001), 'Optimism, pessimism, and psychological well-being', in E. C. Chang (ed.), *Optimism & Pessimism: Implications for Theory, Research, and Practice*, Washington, DC: American Psychological Association, pp. 189–216.

86 G. Melios et al. (2023), 'Les Misérables: An analysis of low SWB across the world', *Frontiers in Psychology* 14: 1107939.

87 K. G. Lockwood et al. (2018), 'Perceived discrimination and cardiovascular health disparities: A multisystem review and health neuroscience perspective', *Annals of the New York Academy of Sciences* 1428(1): 170–207.

88 M. Trent et al. (2019), 'The impact of racism on child and adolescent health', *Pediatrics* 144(2): e20191765.

89 K. M. DeNeve and H. Cooper, H. (1998), 'The happy personality:

A meta-analysis of 137 personality traits and subjective well-being',
Psychological Bulletin 124(2): 197.

90   R. Dong and S. G. Ni (2020), 'Openness to experience, extraversion,
and subjective well-being among Chinese college students: The
mediating role of dispositional awe', *Psychological Reports* 123(3): 903–28.

91   L. B. Spanierman and M. J. Heppner (2004), 'Psychosocial Costs of
Racism to Whites scale (PCRW): Construction and initial validation',
Journal of Counseling Psychology 51(2): 249.

92   L. Blackman (2007), 'Is happiness contagious?', *New Formations* 63: 15.

93   A. C. North, D. J. Hargreaves and J. McKendrick (1999), 'The influence
of in-store music on wine selections', *Journal of Applied Psychology* 84(2):
271.

94   D. Kahneman and J. Renshon (2015), 'Why hawks win', in R. Betts
(ed.), *Conflict After the Cold War*, London: Routledge.

95   S. A. Birch, R. L. Severson and A. Baimel (2020), 'Children's
understanding of when a person's confidence and hesitancy is a cue to
their credibility', *PloS One* 15(1): e0227026.

96   T. Curran (2023), *The Perfection Trap: Embracing the Power of Good Enough*,
New York: Simon & Schuster.

97   D. L. Paulhus and K. M. Williams (2002), 'The dark triad of personality:
Narcissism, Machiavellianism, and psychopathy', *Journal of Research in
Personality* 36(6): 556–63.

98   J. M. Twenge and W. K. Campbell (2009), *The Narcissism Epidemic:
Living in the Age of Entitlement*, New York: Simon & Schuster.

99   C. M. Eddy (2023), 'Self-serving social strategies: A systematic review
of social cognition in narcissism', *Current Psychology* 42: 4362–80, https://
doi.org/10.1007/s12144-021-01661-3.

PART 2: BREAKING SIDES

1   H. J. Walberg and S. L. Tsai (1983), 'Matthew effects in education',
American Educational Research Journal 20(3): 359–73.

2   J. F. Milem (2003), 'The educational benefits of diversity: Evidence
from multiple sectors', in M. J. Chang et al. (eds), *Compelling Interest:
Examining the Evidence on Racial Dynamics in Higher Education*,
Stanford: Stanford Education, pp.126–69, www.researchgate.net/
publication/238506813_The_Educational_Benefits_of_Diversity_
Evidence_from_Multiple_Sectors.

3   P. Dolan et al. (2012), 'Influencing financial behavior: From changing
minds to changing contexts', *Journal of Behavioral Finance* 13(2): 126–42.

4   M. S. Levendusky (2018), 'Americans, not partisans: Can priming
American national identity reduce affective polarization?', *Journal of
Politics* 80(1): 59–70.

5   E. L. Paluck (2009), 'Reducing intergroup prejudice and conflict using
    the media: A field experiment in Rwanda', *Journal of Personality and Social
    Psychology* 96(3): 574.

6   A. D. Galinsky et al. (2008), 'Why it pays to get inside the head of your
    opponent: The differential effects of perspective taking and empathy in
    negotiations', *Psychological Science* 19(4): 378–84.

7   T. K. Vescio, G. B. Sechrist and M. P. Paolucci (2003), 'Perspective taking
    and prejudice reduction: The mediational role of empathy arousal and
    situational attributions', *European Journal of Social Psychology* 33(4): 455–72.

8   C. A. Bail et al. (2018), 'Exposure to opposing views on social media
    can increase political polarization', *Proceedings of the National Academy of
    Sciences* 115(37): 9216–21.

9   M. S. Levendusky (2013), 'Why do partisan media polarize viewers?',
    American Journal of Political Science 57(3): 611–23.

10 D. J. Simons and C. F. Chabris (1999), 'Gorillas in our midst: Sustained
    inattentional blindness for dynamic events', *Perception* 28(9): 1059–74,
    https://doi.org/10.1068/p281059.

11 R. Clay-Williams and L. Colligan (2015), 'Back to basics: Checklists in
    aviation and healthcare', *BMJ Quality & Safety* 24(7): 428–31.

12 Ø. Thomassen et al. (2014), 'The effects of safety checklists in medicine:
    A systematic review', *Acta Anaesthesiologica Scandinavica* 58(1): 5–18.

13 P. Dolan et al. (2012), 'Influencing behaviour: The MINDSPACE way',
    Journal of Economic Psychology 33(1): 264–77.

14 P. Dolan (2020), *Happy Ever After: A Radical Approach to Living Well*,
    London: Penguin, pp. 78–81.

15 D. S. Yeager et al. (2019), 'A national experiment reveals where a growth
    mindset improves achievement', *Nature* 573(7774): 364–69.

16 B. N. Macnamara and A. P. Burgoyne (2023), 'Do growth mindset
    interventions impact students' academic achievement? A systematic
    review and meta-analysis with recommendations for best practices',
    Psychological Bulletin 149(3–4): 133–73, https://doi.org/10.1037/
    bul0000352.

17 J. L. Burnette et al. (2023), 'A systematic review and meta-analysis of
    growth mindset interventions: For whom, how, and why might such
    interventions work?', *Psychological Bulletin* 149(3–4): 174–205, https://doi.
    org/10.1037/bul0000368.

18 M. C. Bligh, J. C. Kohles and Q. Yan (2018), 'Leading and learning to
    change: the role of leadership style and mindset in error learning and
    organizational change', *Journal of Change Management* 18(2): 116–41.

19 P. Dolan et al. (2012), 'Influencing behaviour: The MINDSPACE
    way', *Journal of Economic Psychology*, 33(1): 264–77; P. Dolan et al. (2010),
    'MINDSPACE: influencing behaviour for public policy', Institute for
    Government, www.instituteforgovernment.org.uk/publication/report/
    mindspace (accessed 12 August 2024).

20 J. G. Voelkel et al. (2023), 'Megastudy identifying effective interventions to strengthen Americans' democratic attitudes', https://osf.io/preprints/osf/y79u5 (accessed 12 August 2024).

21 E. DeFilippis (2023), 'Bridging political divides with a cooperative online quiz game', doctoral dissertation, Harvard University Graduate School of Arts and Sciences.

22 D. J. Ahler and G. Sood (2018), 'The parties in our heads: Misperceptions about party composition and their consequences', *Journal of Politics* 80(3): 964–81.

23 B. W. Pelham, M. C. Mirenberg and J. T. Jones (2002), 'Why Susie sells seashells by the seashore: Implicit egotism and major life decisions', *Journal of Personality and Social Psychology* 82(4): 469; J. T. Jones et al. (2004), 'How do I love thee? Let me count the Js: Implicit egotism and interpersonal attraction', *Journal of Personality and Social Psychology* 87(5): 665.

24 I. Soria-Donlan (n.d.), 'In Place of War: Mobilising, empowering and connecting artists in sites of war, revolution and conflict', https://www.academia.edu/11050373/In_Place_of_War_Mobilising_connecting_and_empowering_artists_in_sites_of_war_revolution_and_conflict (accessed 12 August 2024).

25 A. R. Harvey (2020), 'Links between the neurobiology of oxytocin and human musicality', *Frontiers in Human Neuroscience* 14: 350.

26 Daybreaker, 2024. Wake Up & Dance. Available at: https://www.daybreaker.com/ [Accessed 2 September 2024].

27 Belong Center, 2024. Belong Center. Available at: https://www.belongcenter.org/ [Accessed 2 September 2024].

28 B. Tuohey and B. Cognato (2011), 'PeacePlayers International: A case study on the use of sport as a tool for conflict transformation', *SAIS Review of International Affairs* 31: 51.

29 N. Nir and E. Halperin (2019), 'Effects of humor on intergroup communication in intractable conflicts: Using humor in an intergroup appeal facilitates stronger agreement between groups and a greater willingness to compromise', *Political Psychology* 40(3): 467–85.

30 S. E. Torok, R. F. McMorris and W. C. Lin (2004), 'Is humor an appreciated teaching tool? Perceptions of professors' teaching styles and use of humor', *College Teaching* 52(1): 14–20.

31 C. Rosenberg et al. (2021), 'Humor in workplace leadership: A systematic review scoping review', *Frontiers in Psychology* 12: 610795.

32 M. Wanzer, M. Booth-Butterfield and S. Booth-Butterfield (2005), '"If we didn't use humor, we'd cry": Humorous coping communication in health care settings', *Journal of Health Communication* 10(2): 105–25.

33 F. Jiang et al. (2020), 'Does the relation between humor styles and subjective well-being vary across culture and age? A meta-analysis', *Frontiers in Psychology* 11: 2213.

34   M. Feinberg and R. Willer (2015), 'From gulf to bridge: When do moral arguments facilitate political influence?', *Personality and Social Psychology Bulletin* 41(12): 1665–81.

35   M. Kardas, A. Kumar and N. Epley (2022), 'Overly shallow?: Miscalibrated expectations create a barrier to deeper conversation', *Journal of Personality and Social Psychology* 122(3): 367.

36   A. Bechara et al. (1997), 'Deciding advantageously before knowing the advantageous strategy', *Science* 275(5304): 1293–5.

37   B. M. Wagar and P. Thagard (2004), 'Spiking Phineas Gage: A neurocomputational theory of cognitive-affective integration in decision making', *Psychological Review* 111(1): 67.

38   M. T. Richins et al. (2021), 'Incidental fear reduces empathy for an out-group's pain', *Emotion* 21(3): 536.

39   J. Berger and K. L. Milkman (2012), 'What makes online content viral?', *Journal of Marketing Research* 49(2): 192–205.

40   C. Duhigg (2024), *Supercommunicators: How to Unlock the Secret Language of Connection*, New York: Random House.

41   H. Y. Tng and A. K. Au (2014), 'Strategic display of anger and happiness in negotiation: The moderating role of perceived authenticity', *Negotiation Journal* 30(3): 301–27.

42   D. C. Tice, E. Bratslavsky and R. F. Baumeister (2018), 'Emotional distress regulation takes precedence over impulse control: If you feel bad, do it!', in R. F. Baumeister, *Self-regulation and self-control*, London: Routledge, pp. 267–98.

43   F. Harinck and C. K. De Dreu (2008), 'Take a break! or not? The impact of mindsets during breaks on negotiation processes and outcomes', *Journal of Experimental Social Psychology* 44(2): 397–404.

44   G. Loewenstein (2005), 'Hot–cold empathy gaps and medical decision making', *Health Psychology* 24(4S): S49.

45   T. F. Denson, M. L. Moulds and J. R. Grisham (2012), 'The effects of analytical rumination, reappraisal, and distraction on anger experience', *Behavior Therapy* 43(2): 355–64.

46   D. R. Berry et al. (2020), 'Does mindfulness training without explicit ethics-based instruction promote prosocial behaviors? A meta-analysis', *Personality and Social Psychology Bulletin* 46(8): 1247–69.

47   X. Ma et al. (2017), 'The effect of diaphragmatic breathing on attention, negative affect and stress in healthy adults', *Frontiers in Psychology* 8: 234806.

48   J. A. Minson, F. S. Chen and C. H. Tinsley (2020), 'Why won't you listen to me? Measuring receptiveness to opposing views', *Management Science* 66(7): 3069–94.

49   J. J. Chen, L. Xie and S. Zhou (2020), 'Managerial multi-tasking, team diversity, and mutual fund performance', *Journal of Corporate Finance* 65: 101766.

50 Y. Ponomareva et al. (2022), 'Cultural diversity in top management teams: Review and agenda for future research', *Journal of World Business* 57(4): 101328.

51 K. W. Phillips, G. B. Northcraft and M. A. Neale (2006), 'Surface-level diversity and decision-making in groups: When does deep-level similarity help?', *Group Processes & Intergroup Relations* 9(4): 467–82.

52 C. P. Fernandez (2007), 'Creating thought diversity: The antidote to group think', *Journal of Public Health Management and Practice* 13(6): 670–1.

53 T. Karran and L. Mallinson (2017), 'Academic freedom in the UK: Legal and normative protection in a comparative context', report for the University and College Union, www.ucu.org.uk/media/8614/Academic-Freedom-in-the-UK-Legal-and-Normative-Protection-in-a-Comparative-Context-Report-for-UCU-Terence-Karran-and-Lucy-Mallinson-May-17/pdf/ucu_academicfreedomstudy_report_may17.pdf (accessed 12 August 2024).

54 B. Mellers, R. Hertwig and D. Kahneman (2001), 'Do frequency representations eliminate conjunction effects? An exercise in adversarial collaboration', *Psychological Science* 12(4): 269–75.

55 A. L. Mello and J. R. Rentsch (2015), 'Cognitive diversity in teams: A multidisciplinary review', *Small Group Research* 46(6): 623–58.

56 F. Dong et al. (2021), 'The development and validation of a cognitive diversity scale for Chinese academic research teams', *Frontiers in Psychology* 12: 687179.

57 B. L. Kirkman et al. (2004), 'The impact of team empowerment on virtual team performance: The moderating role of face-to-face interaction', *Academy of Management Journal* 47(2): 175–92.

58 N. W. Kohn and S. M. Smith (2011), 'Collaborative fixation: Effects of others' ideas on brainstorming', *Applied Cognitive Psychology* 25(3): 359–71.

59 G. W. Allport (1954), *The Nature of Prejudice*, Reading, MA: Addison-Wesley.

60 D. S. Crystal, M. Killen and M. Ruck (2008), 'It is who you know that counts: Intergroup contact and judgments about race-based exclusion', *British Journal of Developmental Psychology* 26(1): 51–70.

61 T. F. Pettigrew and L. R. Tropp (2006), 'A meta-analytic test of intergroup contact theory', *Journal of Personality and Social Psychology* 90(5): 751.

62 J. Tygiel (1983), *Baseball's Great Experiment: Jackie Robinson and His Legacy*, Oxford: Oxford University Press.

63 G. Lemmer and U. Wagner (2015), 'Can we really reduce ethnic prejudice outside the lab? A meta-analysis of direct and indirect contact interventions', *European Journal of Social Psychology* 45(2): 152–68.

64 L. Bursztyn et al. (2021), 'The immigrant next door: Long-term contact, generosity, and prejudice', National Bureau of Economic Research Working Paper No. w28448.

65   R. Brown and M. Hewstone (2005), 'An integrative theory of intergroup contact', *Advances in Experimental Social Psychology* 37(37): 255–343.

66   T. F. Pettigrew and L. R. Tropp (2006), 'A meta-analytic test of intergroup contact theory', *Journal of Personality and Social Psychology* 90(5): 751–83.

67   M. Sherif (2015), *Group Conflict and Co-operation: Their Social Psychology*, London and New York: Psychology Press.

68   E. M. Uslaner and M. Brown (2005), 'Inequality, trust, and civic engagement', *American Politics Research* 33(6): 868–94.

69   M. Tassinari, M. B. Aulbach and I. Jasinskaja-Lahti (2022), 'Investigating the influence of intergroup contact in virtual reality on empathy: An exploratory study using AltspaceVR', *Frontiers in Psychology* 12: 815497.

70   C. Imperato and T. Mancini (2021), 'Intergroup dialogues in the landscape of digital societies: How does the dialogical self affect intercultural relations in online contexts?', *Societies* 11(3): 84.

71   S. Schumann and Y. Moore (2022), 'What can be achieved with online intergroup contact interventions? Assessing long-term attitude, knowledge, and behaviour change', *Analyses of Social Issues and Public Policy* 22(3): 1072–91.

72   S. B. Hobolt, K. Lawall and J. Tilley (2023), 'The polarizing effect of partisan echo chambers', *American Political Science Review*, pp. 1–16, www.cambridge.org/core/journals/american-political-science-review/article/polarizing-effect-of-partisan-echo-chambers/5044B63A13A458A97CA747E9DCA07228 (accessed 14 August 2024).

PART 3: PICKING SIDES

1   R. N. Smart (1958), 'Negative utilitarianism', *Mind* 67(268): 542–3.

2   A. Williams and R. Cookson (2000), 'Equity in health', in A. J. Culyer and J. P. Newhouse (eds), *Handbook of Health Economics*, Amsterdam: Elsevier, Vol. 1, Part B, pp. 1863–910.

3   P. Dolan and A. Tsuchiya (2009), 'The social welfare function and individual responsibility: Some theoretical issues and empirical evidence', *Journal of Health Economics* 28(1): 210–20.

4   R. Dworkin (2000), *Sovereign Virtue: The Theory and Practice of Equality*, Cambridge, MA: Harvard University Press.

5   P. Foot (2002), *Virtues and Vices and Other Essays in Moral Philosophy*, Oxford: Oxford University Press.

6   S. Flèche and R. Layard (2017), 'Do more of those in misery suffer from poverty, unemployment or mental illness?', *Kyklos* 70(1): 27–41.

7   T. Brown (2023), 'Child poverty: Statistics, causes and the UK's policy response', UK Parliament House of Lords Library, https://lordslibrary.

parliament.uk/child-poverty-statistics-causes-and-the-uks-policy-response/ (accessed 12 August 2024).

8   E. Saez and G. Zucman (2016), 'Wealth inequality in the United States since 1913: Evidence from capitalized income tax data', *Quarterly Journal of Economics* 131(2): 519–78; G. Auten and D. Splinter (2024), 'Income inequality in the United States: Using tax data to measure long-term trends', *Journal of Political Economy*, forthcoming.

9   R. T. Pedersen and D. C. Mutz (2019), 'Attitudes toward economic inequality: The illusory agreement', *Political Science Research and Methods* 7(4): 835–51.

10 R. F. Baumeister and L. E. Brewer (2012), 'Believing versus disbelieving in free will: Correlates and consequences', *Social and Personality Psychology Compass* 6(10): 736–45.

11 P. K. Piff et al. (2010), 'Having less, giving more: The influence of social class on prosocial behavior', *Journal of Personality and Social Psychology* 99(5): 771.

12 I. Robeyns (2022), 'Why limitarianism', *Journal of Political Philosophy* 30(2): 249–70.

13 H. Quilter-Pinner et al. (2022), 'Closing the gap: Parliament, representation and the working class', IPPR, www.ippr.org/research/publications/closing-the-gap (accessed 12 August 2024).

14 M. A. Elkjær and M. B. Klitgaard (2024), 'Economic inequality and political responsiveness: A systematic review', *Perspectives on Politics* 22(2): 318–37, https://doi.org/10.1017/S1537592721002188.

15 M. W. Kraus and D. Keltner (2009), 'Signs of socioeconomic status: A thin-slicing approach', *Psychological Science* 20(1): 99–106.

16 J. Andreoni and R. Petrie (2004), 'Public goods experiments without confidentiality: A glimpse into fund-raising', *Journal of Public Economics* 88(7–8): 1605–23.

17 G. Gulino and F. Masera (2023), 'Contagious dishonesty: Corruption scandals and supermarket theft', *American Economic Journal: Applied Economics* 15(4): 218–51.

18 R. Henderson (2023), *Troubled: A Memoir of Foster Care, Family, and Social Class*, New York: Gallery Books.

19 P. Turchin (2023), *End Times: Elites, Counter-elites, and the Path of Political Disintegration*, London: Penguin.

20 G. J. Borjas (2019), 'Immigration and economic growth', National Bureau of Economic Research Working Paper No. 25836.

21 P. M. Orrenius and M. Zavodny (2007), 'Does immigration affect wages? A look at occupation-level evidence', *Labour Economics* 14(5): 757–73.

22 R. D. Putnam (2007), 'E pluribus unum: Diversity and community in the twenty-first century. The 2006 Johan Skytte Prize Lecture', *Scandinavian Political Studies* 30(2): 137–74.

23   M. Young and P. Wilmott (2013), *Family and Kinship in East London*, London: Routledge.

24   Office for National Statistics (ONS), released 29 November 2022, ONS website, statistical bulletin, Ethnic group, England and Wales: Census 2021.

25   M. V. Cuibus (2024), 'Migrants in the UK: An Overview', Migration Observatory briefing, COMPAS, University of Oxford

26   A. D. Galinsky, G. Ku and C. S. Wang (2005), 'Perspective-taking and self-other overlap: Fostering social bonds and facilitating social coordination', *Group Processes & Intergroup Relations* 8(2): 109–24.

27   J. Brouwer, M. van der Woude and J. van der Leun (2017), 'Framing migration and the process of crimmigration: A systematic analysis of the media representation of unauthorized immigrants in the Netherlands', *European Journal of Criminology* 14(1): 100–19.

28   www.youtube.com/watch?v=6KVO378tjsw (accessed 12 August 2024).

29   A. Bilal and D. R. Känzig (2024), 'The macroeconomic impact of climate change: Global vs. local temperature', National Bureau of Economic Research Working Paper No. w32450.

30   S. Venghaus, M. Henseleit and M. Belka (2022), 'The impact of climate change awareness on behavioral changes in Germany: Changing minds or changing behavior?', *Energy, Sustainability and Society* 12(1): 8.

31   P. Dolan and M. M. Galizzi (2015), 'Like ripples on a pond: Behavioral spillovers and their implications for research and policy', *Journal of Economic Psychology* 47: 1–16.

32   A. U. Ahmed et al. (2007), 'The world's most deprived: Characteristics and causes of extreme poverty and hunger', International Food Policy Research Institute Discussion Paper No. 43.

33   B. C. O'Neill et al. (2010), 'Global demographic trends and future carbon emissions', *Proceedings of the National Academy of Sciences* 107(41): 17521–6.

34   P. Singer (2017), 'Famine, affluence, and morality', in Larry May (ed.), *Applied Ethics*, 6th edition, London: Routledge, pp. 132–42.

35   N. H. Stern (2007), *The Economics of Climate Change: The Stern Review*, Cambridge: Cambridge University Press.

36   S. Elstub et al. (2021), 'The scope of climate assemblies: Lessons from the Climate Assembly UK', *Sustainability* 13(20): 11272.

37   World Economic Forum (2023), '5 environmental scientists tackling climate change', www.weforum.org/agenda/2023/03/5-environmental-scientists-tackling-climate-change/ (accessed 22 July 2024).

38   P. T. Brown et al. (2023), 'Climate warming increases extreme daily wildfire growth risk in California', *Nature*, 621(7980): 760–6.

39   R. McSweeney and A. Tandon (2023), 'Factcheck: Scientists pour cold water on claims of "journal bias" by author of wildfires study', Carbon Brief, 8 September, www.carbonbrief.org/

factcheck-scientists-pour-cold-water-on-claims-of-journal-bias-by-author-of-wildfires-study/ (accessed 12 August 2024).

40 Offences Against the Person Act 1861; Public Order Act 1986, Section 4A; Communications Act 2003, Section 127.

41 www.youtube.com/watch?v=gwgFBFJ6xJc&ab_channel=TotallyBro (accessed 12 August 2024).

42 H. Coyle and PA Media (2023), 'Leeds student jailed for harassment and death threats', BBC News, 10 August, www.bbc.co.uk/news/uk-england-leeds-66462895.

43 M. Smith (2021), 'Cancel culture: What views are Britons afraid to express?', YouGov, 22 December.

44 J. Poushter (2015), '40% of Millennials OK with limiting speech offensive to minorities', Pew Research Center, 20 November, www.pewresearch.org/short-reads/2015/11/20/40-of-millennials-ok-with-limiting-speech-offensive-to-minorities/ (12 August 2024).

45 *Douglas Is Cancelled*, episode 1 (ITV, 2024), written by Steven Moffat, produced by Hartswood Films.

46 J. Haidt and G. Lukianoff (2018), *The Coddling of the American Mind: How Good Intentions and Bad Ideas Are Setting Up a Generation for Failure*, London: Penguin.

47 E. Harrison (2023), 'BBC denies that Roisin Murphy was removed from 6 Music line-up over puberty blockers row', *Independent*, 13 September, www.independent.co.uk/arts-entertainment/music/news/roisin-murphy-bbc-6-music-trans-b2410439.html (accessed 12 August 2024).

48 UK Parliament (2022), 'Your UK Parliament Awards 2022', www.parliament.uk/get-involved/education-programmes/your-uk-parliament-awards-2022/ (accessed 12 August 2024).

49 G. R. Greer and R. Tolbert (1990), 'The therapeutic use of MDMA', in *Ecstasy: The clinical, pharmacological and neurotoxological effects of the drug MDMA*, Boston, MA: Springer US, pp. 21–35.

50 K. D. Brownell et al. (2009), 'The public health and economic benefits of taxing sugar-sweetened beverages', *New England Journal of Medicine* 361(16): 1599.

51 M. Thavorncharoensap et al. (2009), 'The economic impact of alcohol consumption: A systematic review', *Substance Abuse Treatment, Prevention, and Policy* 4: 1–11.

52 C. L. Hart (2022), *Drug Use for Grown-ups: Chasing Liberty in the Land of Fear*, London: Penguin.

53 P. Dolan (2020), *Happy Ever After: A Radical Approach to Living Well*, London: Penguin.

54 M. Cimons (2023), 'Weight-loss drugs Wegovy and Ozempic have unsettling side effects, patients say', *Washington Post*, 8 August, www.washingtonpost.com/health/2023/08/08/weight-loss-drugs-side-effects-wegovy-ozempic/ (accessed 12 August 2024).

55   M. Lindeboom, P. Lundborg and B. van der Klaauw (2010), 'Assessing the impact of obesity on labor market outcomes', *Economics & Human Biology* 8(3): 309–19.

56   B. L. Fredrickson (2004), 'The broaden-and-build theory of positive emotions', *Philosophical Transactions of the Royal Society of London. Series B: Biological Sciences* 359(1449): 1367–77.

57   M. A. M. Peluso and L. H. S. G. De Andrade (2005), 'Physical activity and mental health: The association between exercise and mood', *Clinics* 60(1): 61–70.

58   A. Sullivan (2022), 'Explainer: How abortion became a divisive issue in US politics', Reuters, 25 June, www.reuters.com/world/us/how-abortion-became-divisive-issue-us-politics-2022-06-24/ (accessed 12 August 2024).

59   B. Riley-Smith (2019), 'UK politicians don't do god but religion matters in this election', CNBC, 11 December, www.cnbc.com/2019/12/11/uk-politicians-dont-do-god-but-religion-matters-in-this-election.html (accessed 12 August 2024).

60   P. Singer (2023), *Animal Liberation Now*, New York: Random House.

61   H. Hartig (2022), 'Wide partisan gaps in abortion attitudes, but opinions in both parties are complicated', Pew Research Center, 6 May, www.pewresearch.org/short-reads/2022/05/06/wide-partisan-gaps-in-abortion-attitudes-but-opinions-in-both-parties-are-complicated/ (accessed 12 August 2024).

62   E. Langford (2024), 'UK voters are majority pro-choice across the political spectrum and support extension of at-home abortion', PoliticsHome, 21 April, www.politicshome.com/news/article/bpas-polling-uk-voters-prochoice-political-spectrum (accessed 14 May 2024).

63   YouGov (2012), 'Limits on abortion time?', 24 January, https://yougov.co.uk/politics/articles/2786-limits-abortion-time (accessed 14 May 2024).

64   D. M. Fergusson, L. J. Horwood and J. M. Boden (2009), 'Reactions to abortion and subsequent mental health', *British Journal of Psychiatry* 195(5): 420–6.

65   S. Singh et al. (2018), *Abortion Worldwide 2017: Uneven Progress and Unequal Access*, New York: Guttmacher Institute.

66   T. F. Pettigrew and L. R. Tropp (2005), 'Allport's intergroup contact hypothesis: Its history and influence', in J. F. Davidio, P. Glick and L. A. Rudman (eds), *On the Nature of Prejudice: Fifty Years after Allport*, Malden and Oxford: Blackwell, pp. 262–77.

67   For a summary of age gradients in such views look at: L. Calahorrano (2013), 'Population aging and individual attitudes toward immigration: Disentangling age, cohort and time effects', *Review of International Economics* 21(2): 342–53; L. C. Hamilton, J. Hartter and E. Bell (2019), 'Generation gaps in US public opinion on renewable energy and climate change', *PloS One* 14(7): e0217608.

68 M. Goodwin (2023), *Values, Voice and Virtue: The New British Politics*, New York: Random House.

69 B. Klein Teeselink and G. Melios (2024), 'Origin of (a)symmetry: the evolution of out-party distrust in the United States', *Journal of Politics*, https://www.journals.uchicago.edu/doi/10.1086/732971

70 J. Graham, J. Haidt and B. A. Nosek (2009), 'Liberals and conservatives rely on different sets of moral foundations', *Journal of Personality and Social Psychology* 96(5): 1029.

71 J. M. Kivikangas et al. (2021), 'Moral foundations and political orientation: Systematic review and meta-analysis', *Psychological Bulletin* 147(1): 55.

72 M. Dimock (2014), 'Political polarization in the American public: How increasing ideological uniformity and partisan antipathy affect politics, compromise and everyday life', Pew Research Center, www.pewresearch.org/politics/2014/06/12/political-polarization-in-the-american-public/ (accessed 12 August 2024).

73 B. Klein Teeselink and G. Melios (2024), 'Origin of (a)symmetry: The evolution of out-party distrust in the United States', *Journal of Politics*, https://www.journals.uchicago.edu/doi/10.1086/732971

74 M. Goodwin (2023), *Values, Voice and Virtue: The New British Politics*, New York: Random House.

75 R. J. Dalton (2018), *Political Realignment: Economics, Culture, and Electoral Change*, Oxford: Oxford University Press.

76 A. S. Manstead (2018), 'The psychology of social class: How socioeconomic status impacts thought, feelings, and behaviour', *British Journal of Social Psychology* 57(2): 267–91.

77 J. Tomasi (2012), *Free Market Fairness*, Princeton: Princeton University Press.

78 A. Williams (1997), 'Intergenerational equity: An exploration of the "fair innings" argument', *Health Economics* 6(2): 117–32.

79 A. Tsuchiya, P. Dolan and R. Shaw (2003), 'Measuring people's preferences regarding ageism in health: Some methodological issues and some fresh evidence', *Social Science & Medicine* 57(4): 687–96.

80 M. Dong, J. W. van Prooijen and P. A. van Lange (2019), 'Self-enhancement in moral hypocrisy: Moral superiority and moral identity are about better appearances', *PloS One* 14(7): e0219382.

Index

Index

Page numbers in *italics* indicate illustrations

children and young adults, 171–2
sexism, 4–5, 166
Singer, Peter, 177–8, 180
situational blindness, 78–9
Skin in the Game (Taleb), 48
smoking, 171–2
social class, 4–5, 10, 111–12, 123, 141–4, 171
  working class, 4, 111–12, 141–4
social housing, 146–7
social media, 32, 40–41, 52–3, 67, 78
social norms, 28–9
  cultural transmission, 29
  shared experiences, 29
  social influence, 29
somatic marker hypothesis, 103
Spain, 52
spillovers, 21–7, 39, 61, 49, 183
  permitting spillovers, 154–5
'splitting', 17–18
sport, 92–3, 118, 131–2, 151
  performance-enhancing drugs, 170–71
status hierarchy, 120
stereotypes, 103, 122
Stern Review on the Economics of Climate Change, 156
Sunak, Rishi, 81
Sunday Times Rich List, 140
super-rich, 49, 140–41
Supercommunicators (Duhigg), 104
Sweden, 34–5

Taleb, Nassim, 48

taxation, 49, 134, 138, 140
technology, 116, 121
Thatcher, Margaret, 39
TikTok, 52
time breaks, 105–7
Times Red Box, The, 89
tolerance/intolerance, 5, 15–16, 20, 185, 188
  'tolerance by design', 68, 73, 121, 136
trans rights, 9
  transphobia, 167
transactive memory system (TMS), 30
Trump, Donald, 58
  assassination attempt, 6–7
Twitter/X, 52, 164

United States, 6–7, 19, 23–4
  abortion debate, 176, 178
  affective polarisation (AP), 34–5, *35*
  civil rights movement, 117
  diversity and, 112
  elections, 58–9, 92
  environment and, 77
  freedom of speech, 163
  mistakes and, 85
  political affiliation, 19, 23–4, 26–7, 33–4, 53, 90–91
  presidential election (2016), 58–9
  presidential election (2024), 92
  racism, 3
  reason and, 98
University and College Union (UCU), 113